CATS

Authorised issue 2001 for
Mixing Medienproduktion GmbH, Neckarsulm, Germany
Translation: Rosetta International, London
Printed in Slovenia

CATS

Playmates with velvet paws

Contents

Cats – our

mysterious pets

Cats have in recent years overtaken dogs as the favourite domestic pet in Britain. With over 7,000,000 animals, there are more cats in our households than any other kind of domestic animal.

There are many reasons for the increased popularity of our feline friends. Cats require minimum care. Because they do not need to be taken outdoors, and because they are very clean and quiet animals, cats can live in almost any kind of home. Also, although cats love the company and affection of people, they can be left on their own during the day while one goes out to work. Another advantage is that the running costs are low, the main expenses being vaccination, food and cat litter. They need no licence and they are not taxed.

Because cats are so affectionate they are ideal pets for older people and those living on their own. A cat creates an atmosphere of warmth, it is playful and entertaining, and very loyal. People soon learn to appreciate this and they are happy to share their home with one or two cats. In fact, if you have two cats in the house, you will never have to worry that the poor cats might be bored. Young people should be aware of a cat's need for company because they are more often out of the house – whether at work or out with friends in the evening.

A single cat will often be a better choice for older people who do not go out so much. They will be in to keep it company. Cats do require providing for and looking after – for instance, buying food and

cleaning the litter tray. Two cats will be twice as expensive and twice as much work, so a single cat would be a saving on both counts.

Children also love cats because they are ideal playmates which adore playing and being cuddled. All cat-lovers will acknowledge the pleasure they derive from stroking a cat sitting on their lap and hearing it purring with delight.

However, in order to prevent the cats from suffering an uncertain fate , children, parents, people on their own and older people should be aware that cats live 15 years on average, a few lucky ones reaching the ripe old age of 20. These sweet animals are not a short-term purchase, because they accompany people through a large part of

their life. Too many people are obviously unaware of this, because there is a sad side to people's attitude to cats: many thousands of cats are abandoned every year and picked up by animal protection societies or taken into animal refuges. Many more become strays living in the wild after simply being thrown out by their owners.

But a domestic cat is not a wild predator which adapts easily to living in the wild. Over time, the cat will have built up a close relationship with the people with whom it lived and it will therefore not be completely ill-equipped to face the dangers of surviving on its own in the outside world. In addition, it will have been damaged psychologically by being thrown out or abandoned.

It is therefore important that people should be aware of their responsibilities when they buy a cat or kitten, and it is a good idea to find out more about the habits, moods and needs of cats from a book such as this before you buy one.

All cat lovers who own or want to own a cat will find valuable information in this book that will help them care for their cats. It will tell them about cats' likes and dislikes, explain their personality and give advice in the event of illness or disease.

This book also contains an overall survey of the most prominent breeds, with many colour illustrations. These will give you an idea of the variety and beauty of our mysterious feline friends and the behaviour specific to each breed.

Besides the practical information about cats and how to care for them, there is a section devoted to the cultural history of cats, because the cat has always played an important part in literature, art and film. But their role in the civilisation of man has been an ambivalent one. They have been treated as gods and as useful domestic animals. The cat has also been associated with the powers of evil and mystery, being shunned before eventually being accepted as a loved and irreplaceable member of the household.

When cats became

domestic animals

The evolution of the species

Domestic cats are descended from the Caffre cat, (also known as the African wildcat), and not from the European wildcat

As well as the domestic or house cat which is familiar to everyone, there are 40 or 50 other kinds of cats in the world. Only Australia and Madagascar have no native cats of any kind. Some big and medium-sized cats such as the leopard, jaguar and ocelot, have almost been eradicated through being hunted for their beautiful fur. Most cats are loners but a few species, such as the lion and the feral

The leopard is classed as a big cat while the ocelot is one of the group of small cats. Both have been hunted almost to extinction for their beautiful fur

domestic cat, live in packs.

The cat family can be subdivided into several groups. Big cats include the lion, tiger, leopard and jaguar. The puma, snow leopard, clouded leopard and golden cat are medium-sized cats. The group of small cats includes the ocelot, dwarf tiger cat, Pallas's cat or manul, Geoffroy's cat, pampas cat and wildcats. Finally, lynxes, servals and cheetahs form three further groups.

In the course of the last 8,000 years, one of the small cat species evolved into the domestic cat species of today. The history of the evolution and development of the domestic cat as a species and the similarities revealed in

ancient pictures and carvings demonstrate the relationship between the present house cat (*Felis catus* or *Felis domestica*) and the Caffre cat (*Felis libyca*), also known as the African wildcat or Egyptian wildcat.

The European wildcat (*Felis sylvestris*), which is found in the forests of Slovakia and other parts of central Europe, has a more strongly developed head, body and tail than the African wildcat; the forehead is higher and the tail is strikingly bushy. It is very difficult to tame and domesticate, and the house cat is not descended from it. Even if mated with house cats, the progeny would be wild and untamed.

In contrast the African wildcat has been domesticated for thousands of year in North Africa and the Middle East. The earliest representations of cats have been discovered in the region of Iraq, while the earliest documentary evidence of domesticated cats has been found in Egypt.

However, scientists are not absolutely certain when and where man began including cats in the household, thus starting the process of taming and domestication through which the wildcat evolved into the house cat. It is thought that people adopted cats as domestic animals about 8,000 years ago, at the same time as they began to breed dogs, cattle and sheep for practical purposes. Rock carvings depicting people and animals together show that cats were part of the household entourage. But it is still unclear whether man encountered the cats by chance, or whether they were wildcats caught by man, or if they were an early example of domestic animalsbred on purpose.

Rock paintings of the 6th and 5th century BC found in Jericho show women playing with cats. Similar works have been found in the ancient Sumerian city of Ur, in southern Mesopotamia, situated 150 km (93 miles) west of the present-day city of Basra in Iraq. The rock paintings discovered there are about 4,500 years old. However, it has not

yet been proved that cats were bred as domestic animals in Sumeria and the Middle East.

So far, the earliest reliable proof that cats were bred as

The European wildcat has a much larger head and a more powerful body than the house cat. Like all wild animals it cannot be domesticated

Cats have been appreciated and kept as domestic animals by people for more than 8,000 years

domestic animals in ancient Egypt dates from the 12th and 13th dynasties, about 1800 BC. Archaeological excavations have revealed pictures of cats as well as the mummified remains of young animals, either entombed with the Pharaoh or on their own. So it appears that in that period the Egyptians began to domesticate the African wildcat and keep them in or close by their

dwellings as house pets, taking advantage of their skills in catching rodents.

The cat had been declared a sacred animal several centuries earlier. By 1500 BC cats were not only completely domesticated, but they were also worshipped as divine creatures. This aspect was symbolised by the moon

goddess Bastet or Bast, whom the Egyptians believed was the protector of the home, mother and child. From 1580 BC, she was represented with a cat's head, and bronze or clay statues of cats were produced in her honour. Cats in their thousands were embalmed with the greatest of care as if they were royal mummies and ceremoniously buried in consecrated cat burial grounds such as that of Bubastis in northern Egypt.

In about 400 BC, these skilful catchers of mice and rats had spread throughout the Greek colonies around the Mediterranean, eventually reaching Rome where the inhabitants took them in and looked after them. They soon replaced the less clean, smelly ferrets whose function they

also took over. It was the Romans who gave cats their present name. First called *gatta*, they later became known as *cattus*, from which the French word *chat* is derived, as is the German *Katze*, and of course the English *cat*.

As time went by, cats spread throughout the rest of Europe and Asia Minor where they became popular domestic animals. People recognised their skills and usefulness. They were deified, loved and admired, but also on occasion they were hated, persecuted and killed.

The domestication of cats also spread quite early to Eastern Asia. The house cat was mentioned in Chinese writings as early as 800 BC From there, house cats spread to Japan where they became very popular. From the 10th century onwards they were the object of great veneration at the imperial court where they were looked after with great attention and care.

At this time cats were still accepted in Britain, but this respect and admiration was soon to change. The spread of Christianity brought with it a distrust of these mysterious animals. It was during the Middle Ages that the legends about the negative, magical powers of cats and their association with the devil began. Cats were identified as pagan

This feral house cat does not trust humans. Its ears are flattened and it is ready to pounce if approached

The growing popularity of house cats led to the breeding of pedigree animals, such this handsome pair of Siamese cats

animals, companions and incarnations of the devil. Every disaster and ill which befell people, whether personal misfortune, disease, illness, natural catastrophe or years of drought, were blamed on cats, especially black ones.

This began a period cat persecution all over Europe. In Metz they were burnt and in Flanders they were thrown from the tops of towers. Such gruesome customs survived in many places until the 17th century, and even later cats were still sometimes killed in cruel ways. Superstitious cults still exist today whose members believe that cats are the incarnation of the devil.

The persecution of cats which began in the Middle Ages had dire consequences for people – the disappearance of cats allowed plague epidemics to spread through towns and villages like wild fire. Rats soon took over the towns and villages where

they found food and were able to propagate. This led to plague epidemics such as the Black Death, which spread all over Europe in the 14th century, killing nearly three-quarters of the population.

It was many years before people allowed cats near them again. Cats first re-appeared in manor houses and palaces where they were treated as cuddly pets by the aristocracy. Gradually people began to remember their usefulness as predators, keeping down the population of rats and mice. They protected the crops, the harvest and the farm from unpleasant vermin – indeed their mere presence drove away rats, mice and even insects.

Cats now also became welcome passengers on ships because they were the only way of ensuring that the provisions would not be eaten by rats before they reached their destination. There were cats

on the Mayflower during its voyage to the New World. The early settlers appreciated these domestic animals, first in the countryside where cats acted as pest controllers on farms, and then in the home itself and in the new towns where they began to be

appreciated for the warm, cozy atmosphere they created around them.

The increasingly popular of cats as domestic animals, led to the specific breeding of

The Siamese is one of the best known and most popular cat breeds.

particular breeds satisfying people's aesthetic preferences and practical needs.

The affectionate nature of cats, their magnificent colouring, their great elegance, the tranquillity and peace which emanates from them and their gentleness all contribute to their great popularity as pets.

Today Great Britain and the United States are the most important centres for breeding pedigree cats. Cats have been appreciated in North America since as long ago as 1626, and today people in the United States are prepared to pay vast sums for the finest rare pedigree cats.

The first cat show was held in London in 1871, and in subsequent years the animals exhibited came to include exotic breeds such as Siamese cats. Societies devoted to particular breeds were formed first in Britain from 1910 onwards.

The evolution of the house cat as a species depended on the taming of wildcats. Over many generations, the best, least aggressive and least shy have been bred to arrive at the completely domesticated house cats of today. Nonetheless, even after several thousand years of co-existence with humans, they have succeeded in retaining much of their independence. They can be 'trained' a little, but not to the same degree as dogs. They often recognise their name, but real training is out of the question. Cats do not respond to commands and they always follow their own inclinations. Yet many will often look for the company of humans in order to snuggle up against them and be cuddled to satisfy their need for affection.

But there is no absolute guarantee that a cat will be affectionate with its owners and agree to be cuddled, nor will its nature in this respect be apparent immediately – some may even shun the company of humans altogether. Some cats are very shy and only emerge from their cornervery hesitantly. Others prefer playing to being cuddled, and they will always be looking for something to scratch, gnaw or chase. Some refuse to be approached at all and ward off any attempt to come closer by hissing, scratching and biting.

The breeding of pedigree cats

Many different breeds of cats have been developed through careful selective breeding. These vary tremendously in appearance, colour, size and fur type, as well as in behaviour and personality. Almost all these breeds have been bred exclusively as house cats. Some like to go out in the garden, others may venture a little further afield, and a few enjoy roaming through the fields to satisfy their natural hunting instincts.

Even the most affectionate cats are always on their guard. As predators, they are aware of any danger lurking round the corner and they are always ready to retreat.

Scared of water

but agile climbers

Cats are masters of the arts of climbing and balancing ...

The remarkable skills of the cat

Cats are highly developed mammals. The cat's physical skills and strongly developed senses are perfectly geared to the hunting of small prey. The explanation of its great mobility, agility and suppleness is that it has 244 bones and 512 muscles. The vertebrae in the neck, chest and lumbar region are so flexible that the cat can turn and twist from head to toe; it can turn its head 180° to clean itself, it can arch its back to an amazing height, and it can also stretch to an incredible length, when leaping for instance. It has five pads and claws on its front legs and four on its back legs which enable it to walk as if on tiptoes. The hard skin on the pads gives them the necessary frictional quality while the fat cells under the skin of the pads and the dense fur between the toes makes the paws feel like velvet cushions. They also mean that the cat can move without making the slightest noise and pounce on its unsuspecting prey. Their razor-sharp claws, which are turned inward, and the carnassial (sharp-edged) teeth are most effective weapons when hunting small prey. When running and jumping cats retract their claws inside the pouch-shaped pads. In this way the claws are protected because they do not come into contact with the ground – as they do with dogs – and this helps them remain sharp. The cat itself makes sure through daily care that its claws are sharp and ready for action whenever necessary. With the help of a scratching pole or other object, the cat will keep the claws on its front paws in good condition and the right length, but it will use its teeth to take care of the claws on its hind paws.

The cat is a skilled climber and will use its claws to climb up any obstacle, to grab and hold down its prey and to drive away any attacker. A cat's power to defend itself is shown by the great strength of its front legs and the sharpness of the front claws. It can inflict serious damage even on large attackers, and dogs are therefore very wary when they encounter a cat they do not know. The hind legs are even stronger, twice as powerful as the front legs. This

... and they will also display these skills in the home

down. It is quite common for for a cat to need help in descending, and it may even have to be rescued from high places by the fire brigade. This is because they are quite unable to climb backwards. Nor can they climb down head first, because their backward curved claws provide no grip when climbing down.

Fortunately, a fall even from a great height will not usually injure them because of the enormous elasticity and powerful extensors in their limbs. But as a rule cats prefer not to jump down from a height and they will often wait – sometimes for days – for outside assistance to help them down.

An adult cat has 30 teeth, embedded in powerful, flexible jaws. The most important teeth are the four large, powerful carnassials – two at the top and at the bottom. They are used to grab, hold and tear their prey to pieces. Between the carnassials are six small incisors, used mainly for grooming. In addition, the cat has a total of 16 back teeth (six at the top and ten at the bottom) which it uses like scissors to cut up its food, because cats are unable to chew.

A well-aimed leap of 2 metres (over 6 ft) is quite a normal jump for a cat

enables the cat to make enormous leaps: from a standing position it can jump up to five times its body length in any direction. Normally weighing 3–6 kg (6½–13 lbs), it will playfully 'catapult' its body, about 50 cm (20 in) long across cupboards and garage roofs. Before leaping, the cat crouches – it bends the hind legs and then suddenly stretches out. If the target is within reasonable reach, the cat will jump far enough to be able to land on its hind legs. The cat is thus able to reach its planned target and to bring into action its most important stabilising instrument, the tail, as well as using its front legs to support

itself. If the target is too far away, the cat displays a skill which is unique among mammals. Just its front paws reach the target and it then pulls itself up like a gymnast. That is why there are almost no obstacles that a cat cannot overcome. But however good cats are at climbing up and leaping over obstacles, they are very bad at climbing

*Cats are excellent hunters
with their four carnassial teeth*

The 'six' senses of the domestic cat

The cat can make excellent use of its great strength and leaping and climbing skills because all its senses are very strongly developed. Unlike a dog, a cat does not rely mainly on its sense of smell, but uses itis five senses in equal measure. Hearing, seeing, smelling, feeling and tasting are all brought into action when it is is investigating the world around it.

Cat's eyes

Because of its third eyelid (known as the nictitating membrane) in the inner corner of its eyes, a cat does not need to blink constantly to keep its eyes moist. The nictitating membrane ensures the necessary moistening of the eyeball. The cat's surprising ability to keep its large, strikingly coloured eyes wide open without blinking gives it a slightly eerie, enigmatic character. In strong light, the pupils become reduced to a narrow, vertical slit while in the dark the pupils become round and up 12 mm (½ in) across. They can perceive the size and shape of an object with great accuracy, as well as its distance away. Objects from 2 to 6 metres (6 to 20 ft)

Eyes, ears and whiskers help a cat to orientate Itself with accuracy and to locate food and prey with great precision

One of a cat's most beautiful features are its large, shining eyes

*The secret of
a cat's 'sixth
sense' lies in
its vibrissae.
These are
bristly hairs
which grow
around the
mouth and
above the
eyes; they are
sensitive to
temperature
and pressure
as well as
touch*

away are perceived as clearly as they are by humans.

By contrast, cats do not recognise colours as well as humans. They can distinguish between black and white and blue and green, but they confuse red and yellow.

This relatively poor colour recognition is compensated by their great sensitivity to light: light rays are reflected by tissue situated behind the retina which acts like a mirror, so that very low light levels can be perceived. Cats can recognise objects in the dark at a distance of as much as 10 metres (33 ft)as clearly as they can in the light. This double reflection of the light is also the reason why cats' eyes are so and bright even in dim light.

The cat's sense of touch and its 'sixth sense'

Cats owe their excellent sense of touch to its whiskers or vibrissae. They are clearly more bristly than the rest of the cat's hair and they grow on the face and front paws of the cat. These sensitive hairs include the whiskers on the face which are very long and clearly recognizable, the 30 or so moustache- and beard-like hairs along the upper and lower lip, the 12 bristly hairs on the cheeks and above the eyes, and the five sensitive hairs on each of the front paws. These sensitive hairs enable the cat to 'sense' the world around it because these hairs are have powerful roots which are full of sensitive nerves and muscles.

As well as reacting to touch and vibration, these hairs are also sensitive to changes of temperature and air pressure. This is probably the explanation of the scientifically unproven ability of cats to anticipate imminent earthquakes, volcanic eruptions and thunderstorms, and even to register distant explosions. These natural phenomena emit shockwaves which are imperceptible to humans, causing changes in atmospheric pressure which the cat's 'sixth sense' may be able to register.

It is through seeing, touching and smelling that the cat explores the world around it. Every unknown object is first carefully studied by the cat from a safe distance. It then uses its vibrissae to establish the temperature of the object. Only then will it approach and explore it more thoroughly with its nose and paws.

When the cat's highly sensitive eyes are no longer able to pierce the darkness, it will use its organs of touch to orientate itself in the dark, as well as to identify objects and other animals.

*This cat is
using all its
senses so as
not to miss
anything*

The sense of smell

The cat owes its highly developed sense of smell to the 200 million olfactory cells in its mouth and throat. They are constantly busy, grooming themselves, eating and getting to know other creatures. Cats are always sizing up their environment.

In the roof of the mouth there is a specialised olfactory organ, the so-called Jacobson's organ. This small cone helps the cat to identify interesting smells more accurately, particularly when encountering other members of its species. A cat's sense of smell leads it to food and drink, activates the gustatory nerves and stimulates the appetite. That is why a cat with a cold has no appetite and rejects food. The olfactory nerves are particularly sensitive to the smell of valerian and catnip – if you want to attract your cat, try it with these. The gustatory nerves on the tongue and roof of the mouth are able to distinguish between

A cat uses its nose to test what it eats. It will not eat anything which does not smell right

salted, bitter and spicy foods and they also react to sweet foods. But the cat relies much more on its sense of smell than on its sense of taste when choosing food and eating it. If its food does not smell nice to it, a cat will not eat it.

The sense of hearing

Cats' ears are extremely sensitive in perception of vibrations. Their ears can pick up all sounds from 20 up to 25,000 cycles per second (20 Hz to 25 kHz), and they work in association with the organs of touch. The position and great mobility of its ears enables the cat to locate the noises it hears with great accuracy, determining the direction of movement and

speed with precision. This is why a cat can locate even a hidden mouse merely by using its ears. This is because the mouse is continually sending messages to other members of its species using ultrasonic frequencies; these signals are then intercepted by the cat. Its excellent sense of hearing also helps it to orientate itself within its surroundings; familiar sounds are as important as familiar objects in the process of orientation. Indeed, background noises help a cat to form a mental picture of its surroundings and it uses these noises as landmarks. Hearing also helps a cat to recognise familiar events and people. Cats identify the steps and voices of those who live with them with great accuracy. It can therefore recognise people even when it does not see them.

The cat's excellent hearing and its 'pictorial' memory is why so many cats are able to find their home again even from great distances. When setting off, a cat will 'record' mental pictures of its surroundings and it will also commit the background noises to memory. Then it will 'read' these pictures and noises backwards one by one, so as to retrace its journey step by step back to its familiar territory.

The cat also uses its ears to find its way around. It can form an acoustic picture of its surroundings from what it hears

*Right:
This little kitten
has unusually
long whiskers*

A cultural

history of cats

a culinary delicacy and their fur, ashes and urine are believed to have curative properties.

The legends, fairy tales and superstitions linked to cats are probably prompted by their mysterious nature. Their roving eyes glowing in the dark, their sudden soundless appearance out of the shadows, their great individuality, their obvious smugness, their sudden random aggressiveness and their unpleasant habit of 'playing' with their prey make them rather eerie creatures. This could be the explanation for the association of cats with witchcraft and devilry. Indeed, even today cats feature strongly in horror movies and books. But on the other hand, their sociable nature, cuddly qualities, playfulness, purring and ability to arouse affection in us explain why cats are often featured in children's books and films, as well as in stories, novels and poems for adults.

Black cats in particular gave rise to many legends associated with cats

Previous page: Egyptian bronze statuette of a cat with her young

The relationship of people with cats has always been remarkably ambivalent through the ages and in the various civilisations of the world. The relationship has ranged from divine worship in some ancient civilisations to condemnation and persecution in Europe during the Middle Ages. In the course of their chequered history, cats have been seen as symbols of fertility and freedom, and their appearance known as an omen of good fortune or bad luck. In its capacity of mousecatcher, the cat is an economically useful animal, and because of its cuddliness it is a delightful companion. But in some cultures, cats are seen as

Below: An Egyptian bronze of a sacred cat from the 4th century BC

Cats in the past

In the past, animals have played an important part in many civilisations. Because of their mysterious nature and behaviour, cats were ascribed particular powers, often devilish, as well as special abilities to benefit or hurt people.

These powers were countered by magic, either to ward off evil spells or to harness them in a beneficial manner.

This led to expiatory rituals and the prohibition against killing cats for fear of demonic repercussions. The worship of animals in their own right was replaced by the worship of deities, which were however associated with particular animals. The association was based on the properties, abilities, skills and behaviour of the animal and the representation of the nature of the deity they were associated with. In addition, there was the belief that gods were able to take on the shape of certain animals and thus also their cunning, trickery and skills.

In the mythology of ancient Egyptian , the great sun god Re took on the shape of a cat to overcome Apep, the snake of darkness. The goddess Mafdet was another snake-killing deity, and she is represented as the Pharaoh's protector in the form of a cat in some of the wall paintings in the pyramids. The most important figure was the goddess of fertility, Bast or Bastet, who was venerated in the sun temple of Heliopolis; she was represented with either the body or head of a cat. The importance of this goddess was so great that cats enjoyed great veneration throughout Egypt. The centre and place of pilgrimage of this cult of the cat was Bubastis, a sanctuary where temple cats were kept. It was the task of the priests to look after and observe the cats, and from this to interpret the messages of the goddess. If a believer needed help or wanted to make a vow, he

By the 6th century BC cats were worshipped as deities in Egypt. This statuette is of the protective goddess Bastet in the form of a cat

custodians of the cats who used it to look after them.

On a cat's death, whether it was a temple or a house cat, it would be embalmed and buried in a beautifully decorated coffin or sarcophagus. As a sign of mourning, all the members of the family shaved off their eyebrows . In

would cut his child's hair which would be weighed against silver. The silver would then be given to the Bubastis alone archaeologists have discovered over 300,000 mummies of cats in burial chambers; most had probably been brought here from every part of the country.

The cat's position in the life of the ancient Egyptians was so important that the deliberate killing of a cat was punished by death. Even if the cat's death was accidental or caused by careless ness, heavy fines were imposed. The worship of cats was so ingrained

country, whereby for 12 days sacrifices would be offered to the spirit so that the latter would return the offering to the worshipper enhanced and blessed. Many families kept cats as spirits in the house. However, this cult was considered heretical and was forbidden so that it soon disappeared.

dark, negative, feminine element. A tale from the era of the Songs reveals how highly the ancient Chinese thought of the cat's intelligence. The story tells of a wealthy businessman who loved to boast about his precious possessions to his friend: 'Everything in my house is precious and special – only my cat is not special.' The cat immediately stood on its hind legs, put its front paws together in a respectful manner and said, 'I did not want to frighten Your Excellency…'

In Japan cats were originally very rare and therefore highly valued. They were kept by high-ranking personalities at the imperial court, which treated the animals with great respect. This is shown by the story of the cat which had a wet-nurse put at its disposal after giving birth to a litter, or the tale of the tom cat which had an official rank and everything that went it, including a salary, servants and honours.

But since the 14th century, cats have been associated with superstition and demons. Legends spread of sinister changes, where people turning into cats and cats into people. For instance, there is a legend of a vampire cat which killed the mistress of a prince, took her form, and then sucked the prince's blood. Such a cat was represented

Le Chat painted by the Japanese artist Tsugouharu Foujita (1927)

that the Persian king Cambyses succeeded in capturing the Egyptian town Pelusion without any opposition because he ordered his soldiers to hold cats in front of them.

In ancient China during the Sui dynasty, a cat cult known as 'Miau-kuei' developed in some parts of the

Later the cat became a symbol of good luck and long life. In Chinese script, the word 'miao' or 'mao' means 'cat', but it also means 'worthy and old', that is 80 years old, and therefore 'commanding respect'. Because the cat is a nocturnal animal, it is associated with Yin, the

with two tails to represent its demonic nature. Indeed, it was believed that the cat's demonic power was exclusively in the tail, and that without a tail, cats were harmless. This led to cats having their tails cut off and later to the breeding of cats with a stumpy tail, a peculiarity resulting from a genetic mutation.

In India, the cat was also known as ' The Most Perfect' or 'The Unsullied', and it played an important part in religion. According to a legend from Assam, a particular cat first approached a human being when its cousin the tiger was sick and shivering violently. The cat decided to ask a man for fire to warm the tiger. But there was noone in the house and the cat went inside to get the fire for itself. There it found some rice and fish which it could not resist. After eating, the cat rolled up into a ball and was about to go to sleep when it remembered the reason for his visit. It took a piece of burning firewood in its teeth and carried it into the tiger's den. When the tiger had been warmed, the cat declared that it had decided to start a new life and go and live with humans, because there was always plenty of food and warmth there.

The prophet Mohammed, founder of Islam, was also a cat lover. It is said that one day his cat Mussa had fallen asleep on one of the wide sleeves of his burnoose when the Prophet was called to prayer – something which he himself had told his followers to do at particular times of the day. But because he did not want to disturb the sleep of his cat, he cut the sleeve of his garment so as not to disturb the cat in its sleep.

The usefulness of the cat is described in an Islamic variation of the story of the flood. Noah asked a lioness for advice and help because the ark had been invaded by rats and mice. Thereupon the lioness offered Noah the most effective remedy against to rats: she sneezed and 'bore' a couple of kittens from her nostrils.

In contrast with the settled Arabs, nomads saw the cat as an evil demon or jinn. Protection was given by hanging the paw of a black cat from the belt because this would make its wearer identifiable. In the seven books of eastern legends, it is said: 'Jinns love to be around people and often take on the appearance of an animal, because they crave human affection but do not want to be recognised.'

Several other ancient cultures had deities associated

The prophet Mohammed was known for his love of cats. This picture is an illustration of 'The Cat and the Rat', from an Arabic book dating from about 1350

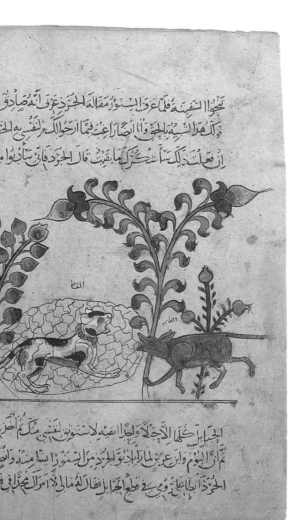

with cats. Thus, the Incas had a cat-like fertility goddess, the Celts had a divinity with a cat's head, and in ancient Germanic mythology Freya's coach was drawn by two cats.

Until the Middle Ages cats were appreciated and highly regarded in Europe. According to a 5th-century legend St Patrick freed Ireland from snakes with the help of cats, while a poem written in the 9th century by an Irish monk further illustrates people's love of cats:

> Pangur, my white tom cat,
> and I, we are both artists.
> He chases mice. I must think
> And bury myself in my books…
> That is how we spend our day.
> We do not disturb each other;
> We each have our friends;
> We each do our own thing…

In Britain the cat's ability to catch mice has long been highly valued and its usefulness was even recognised by the law. For instance, in the 10th century in Wales, a law stated that a village should have nine buildings, a plough, a kiln, a butter churn, a cat, a cockerel, a bull and a shepherd. A cat was valued as much as a calf or the foal of a work horse. If the cat guarded the royal barn, it was even more valuable: 'He who kills a cat which is guarding a house or barn belonging to the king or who abducts it, must hold the cat by the head over a well-swept floor and pour clean wheat until the tip of its tail is covered. That is its value.'

Superstition and common beliefs

The high regard for cats turned into suspicion and hatred at the beginning of the Middle Ages when witch-hunting began to develop in Europe. As superstition and the persecution of witches spread, cats were increasingly seen as the incarnation of the devil or the devil's companion, marked by the devil. A German monk wrote in the 13th century '…they are called heretics because they hide in corners which they find empty, as cats do. No other animal harms man as much as the cat does… Therefore, dear people, chase away cats! Their breath is dangerous… Chase them out of every corner because cats are deadly. As are heretics…'

In the 12th and 13th century the Waldensians and Albigensians were accused of practising rituals involving cats. Members of the Order of the Knights Templar 'confessed' under torture that

Terracotta statuettes of cats have been found in Peru, dating from the 1st to the 6th century

they had worshipped the devil in the form of a black cat. In Metz in 1344, the devil in the shape of a cat was thought to be responsible for an outbreak of St Vitus's dance, and annually for the next 400 years the inhabitants would burn 13 cats locked up in iron cages.

In England, at the coronation of Elizabeth I, live cats were confined in an effigy of the Pope, carried around in procession and finally burnt. Women condemned to death by drowning were put in a sack with a cat before being thrown into the water. Often the mere fact of owning a cat was enough to be accused of witchery and condemned to death. In 1659 Edward Topsell wrote in a serious work on natural history that the 'the companion of witches usually appear in the form of a cat, which clearly explains why these animals are dangerous for the soul and body.'

Cats were thought to be able to climb up chimneys and walk through walls. They allegedly gathered at crossroads take part in the Witches' Dance. and on the Sabbath they acquired iron-clad feet. When houses, walls and dams were built, cats were embedded in the walls to make the building last longer. The protective magic of Saint John's Fire in June was 'strengthened' by the burning of live cats. A manuscript dating from 1286 mentions 'fire cats' which as the name suggests were destined to be burned alive. Special occasions were also celebrated by sacrificing cats. For instance, cats were

Since the Middle Ages cats have been linked with witchcraft. This lithograph entitled The Witch *is by Hans Thoma and dates from 1870*

*Do all cats look grey at night?
It depends – but they certainly
all have luminous eyes!*

burned on Shrove Monday, on Ash Wednesday more cats were killed, while a black cat would be buried alive to mark the beginning of the sowing season. At the end of the season another cat would be killed.

This madness continued for several centuries. The last known official witch trial took place in Switzerland in 1782. The persecution of cats led to the spreading of the plague.

The belief that animals have special inner powers has survived until today. The

*A black cat
coming from
the left is
said to bring
bad luck.
This super-
stition is still
believed by
many people*

ancient representations of deities with animal attributes was undoubtedly responsible for the fact that the characteristic features and behaviour of animals were transferred to human beings, while human traits and mental abilities were ascribed to cats. Their keen eye sight, uncanny instinct and apparent ability to forecast the weather were linked to prophetic skills.

Cats are still thought to be endowed with prophetic skills, such as announcing a visit, prophesying good or bad luck and forecasting the weather. For instance, the cat announces a visit by washing itself from front to back or vice-versa. If it washes himself from the front towards the back, the visitor will be a man, and if it is in the other direction, the visitor will be a woman. If it licks its tail, it will be an unpleasant visit. But if it cleans himself all over, scratches itself with its paw and rubs its nose, a pleasant visit can be expected.

A cat howling announces a quarrel or fight – especially on a Friday night. If a black cat crosses the road, an accidentcan be expected. A black cat should never be struck with the hand because the arm would become paralysed.

If a cat is the first thing seen in the morning or in the New Year, it is good luck. According to an old English

proverb, 'If the house cat is black, there will be no shortage of suitors'.

Cats also appear in many sayings and proverbs:

When the cat's away, the mice will play.
All cats are grey in the dark.
Playing cat and mouse.
First rubbing against you, then scratching. That's what a cat is like.
Sick as a cat
A cat has nine lives.
A cat which has swallowed a canary still cannot sing.
Like a cat on hot bricks.
Letting the cat out of the bag .
All cats love fish but fear to wet their paws.
Enough to make a cat laugh.
To call a cat a cat
To grin like a Cheshire cat.
Horse's hooves, cat's claws and card-players' hands cannot be trusted.
No room to swing a cat.
See how the cat jumps.
Birds who sing too early are caught by the cat at night
When the maid has nibbled, the cat gets a hiding.

If you want to have a long life, eat like a cat and drink like a dog.

Set the cat among the pigeons.

A cat may look at a king.

Raining cats and dogs.

Not a cat in hell's chance.

There are also many words and phrases in which the word 'cat' appears. Examples include calling a spiteful woman 'catty', the game of tipcat, a cat-nap, cat's tongues (chocolate biscuits), cat-o'-nine-tails (a whip with nine knotted thongs), cat lick (a quick wash), and something the cat brought in (bedraggled in appearance).

In Ypres, in Flanders, a cat-throwing competition is still held every two years. Today these are soft toy cats thrown from a watch-tower to the ground, but not very long ago this 'spectacle' was performed with live cats.

Cats and the fine arts

The earliest representations of cats are parts of statuettes of about 6000 BC discovered by archaeologists in Anatolia. These statuettes show women playing with cats and suckling them.

In Egypt, many representations of cats have been found because of the cat's importance in ancient Egypt. These include wall paintings in tombs or statuettes which symbolised the goddess Bastet because of their mythological association with the deity. They are also depicted on numerous mummies and coffins of cats. But there are also representations of cats as a house cats, shown sitting on a lap or under a chair.

On the other hand, hardly any representations of cats from ancient Rome and ancient Greece have been found. This seems to indicate that the many cat-like animals which appear on Greek vases and sculptures are not house-cats but martens or civets.

In China the cat appears in literature and paintings from the 10th century onward. The painter Li-A-Chi who specialised in cats chose themes such as 'Cats playing among plants', 'Drunken cat', 'Birds, cats and toads', 'Cats playing with their young', 'Cats at Play' and 'Angry Cats'. The painter Ho-Tsun-shih was famous for his masterful paintings depicting cats in all positions, often with sunflowers. In the 15th century Tai Chien painted a 'Tom cat chasing butterflies' as a birthday present. In Taoist tradition the same forces control people and nature, so objects represented always have a symbolic meaning as well as a literal one. So here the tom cat is the symbol of venerable old men and the butterfly of even greater old age. This birthday painting is therefore interpreted as 'To the 80-year-old, that he may become a 90-year-old'.

In Japan, cats were usually represented with a stumpy

Three little toy cats from Japan

tail in paintings and woodcuts. The reason for this was the fear which existed even then of the demonic power in the cat's tail. They were only represented with a tail or a double tail if they symbolised demons or vampire cats.

In Europe, pictures of cats only appeared later. The persecution of witches gave rise to a large number of paintings, drawings and woodcuts in which cats were shown as witches' familiars, or representing witches who had turned into cats or incarnations of the devil.

But by the 15th century Leonardo da Vinci was producing studies of the movement of cats without demonising them. In his drawings he shows cats crawling, lying in wait, chasing things, hunting, playing, cleaning themselves, cowering, arching their back, hissing and snarling. Albrecht Dürer in his engraving *The Fall of Man* drew Adam and Eve with a cat at their feet. The Flemish painter Pieter Breughel the Elder painted *A Concert of Cats*. In the 16th century, the Venetian painter Tintoretto also included cats in several of his mannerist paintings. In the 17th century the Dutch painter Jan Steen, known for his humorous caricature-like genre paintings of working people, made a painting called *The Reading Hour* of three children trying to teach their cat to read. The French painter Jean Antoine Watteau (1684–1721), famous for his paintings of *fêtes champêtres*, also painted *The Sick Cat'* in Rococo style.

In the 18th century the increasingly wealthy bourgeoisie began to overtake the aristocracy as patrons of the arts. They started having portraits painted of them and their families, often including their children with domestic animals such as cats. Examples include portraits of *Eugène de Baculard d'Arnaud* by Jean-Baptiste Greuze, *Gabrielle Arnaud as a Child* by Louis Léopold Boilly and *Louise Vernet as Child* by Théodore Géricault.

The portrait of *Don Manuel Osorio de Zuñiga with his Cats and Birds* commissioned from Francisco José de Goya y Lucientes depicts cats as demonic creatures, the forerunners of his witch's cats in his series of etchings *Los Caprichos*. The pictorial broadsheet *How the Mice Buried the Cats* in which the cat is represented as a defeated tyrant had a tremendous success. Other broadsheets showed how mice stormed the cats' fortress. The mice are always depicted as an unfortunate, subjugated minority while the cat always symbolises tyranny.

The Impressionists of the late 19th century knew how to exploit the mysterious, romantic symbolism surrounding cats. Edouard Manet painted the *Woman with a Cat on her Lap* and *The Listening Cat* while Jean Renoir painted *Woman with*

Cat and *Girl with Cat*. Art Nouveau artists also included the cat as a subject in their paintings: artists such as the Swiss painter Felix Valloton with *Girl playing with a Cat*, the British artist Aubrey Beardsley's *Black Cat* and th French artist Émile Gallé, celebrated for his magnificent glassware, who also made a beautiful glazed clay cat. Even Henri de Toulouse-Lautrec

who specialised in paintings and posters showing the ladies of the Paris demimonde, produced a portrait of *Kitten Minette*.

The cat continued as a popular subject in the 20th century. Franz Marc painted *The White Cat*, depicted lying on a yellow cushion. In Max Beckmann's etching *The Evening* Frau Battenberg is seen with a cat on her lap, while in his

Franz Marc's **The White Cat***, dating from 1912*

Théophile A. Steinlein's picture Stretched-out Cat *is in the Musée du Petit Palais in Geneva*

woodcut *Woman with Candle*, a cat is shown sitting on the window sill. His *Self-Portrait with a Hard Hat* is interesting in that the cat is placed in an empty background as an idol figure. Ludwig Kirchner produced a woodcut of his tomcat Bobby and called it *Sleeping Cat* while Paul Klee produced *Monologue of a Kitten*. The cat appears as a mysterious creature in Maurice Sendak's *The Enigmatic Cat*.

The author and illustrator also created the famous children's book *Where the Wild Things Are*. The behaviour of cats in *Cat and Bird* by caricaturist Olaf Gulbransson is very ambivalent, while the cat in the *Cat on the Stairs* is part of a cycle of woodcuts created by Frans Masereel as a story told in pictures without words. Pablo Picasso found cats the most considerate, thoughtful, attentive

company but he was also aware of their wild side; his representation of *Cat Catching a Bird* is fairly gruesome. On the other hand, he was equally aware of the erotic symbolism of cats and used it very effectively in his drawing *Woman and Cat*.

The list of known and lesser known artists who have represented cats in their work is endless. Théophile Alexandre Steinlen was able to paint

a perfect picture of a cat and also to express its nature. Another excellent artist is Gottfried Mind, the 'Raphael of Cats', whose illustrations are quite captivating.

But the 'king' among artists depicting cats was undoubtedly Louis Wain. H. G. Wells said that he had created his own individual style of cat, a world of cats such that English cats had to look like Wain cats. Naive artists such as Max Raffler, Morris Hirschfield, Jan Balet and Kathia Berger also made many pictures of cats.

Last but not least, there are the many innovative creators of children's books, such as Beatrix Potter with *The Tale of Tom Kitten*, Kathleen Hale (creator of *Orlando the Marmalade Cat*), and Nicola Bayley, who all succeed in never trivialising cats in their books.

The French novelist Théophile Gauthier had some 25 cats himself, and he wrote: 'To paint a cat, you require genius'. Plenty have tried and a remarkable number have succeeded.

The cat as a character in films and literature

It is thought that in ancient Egypt there were many stories, poems and songs about cats but none of them have survived. The seven books of Eastern sagas which appeared very much later were already known. There were also many Chinese stories, legends and anecdotes about cats and Japanese writers and story-writers who included cats in their writings.

In the 6th century BC the cat reappeared in Western literature in the Greek author Aesop's fables. In 'The Cat and the Cockerel', 'The Bat and the Cat' and in 'The Town-mouse and the Field Mouse' the cat is shown as having a rather bad reputation. It is two-faced, deceitful and eats its guests. The Greek historian Herodotus visited the town of Bubastis in 450 BC and he wrote that he was rather taken aback by the Egyptians' great love of cats, which seemed rather ridiculous to him. Indeed, in a Greek play one of the characters makes fun of the Egyptians' love of cats.

Herodotus also reported that tom cats would snatch kittens away from their mother and kill them so as to have a chance to mate again. This belief was so strongly ingrained that as late as the 16th century the Swiss physician and naturalist Conrad Gesner wrote in his five-volume work on zoology *Historiae Animalium* (1551–87) that tom cats were 'nest robbers'. Even in the 17th century science and legend were often confused, as shown for example by Edward Topsell, mentioned earlier. One hundred years later, Georges Louis Buffon wrote in his *Histoire naturelle* that cats were 'disloyal servants' and that 'people only keep cats out of necessity in order to get rid of an even more unpleasant animal... Moreover, they are endowed with an innately evil, stubborn and treacherous nature.'

Alfred Brehm was the first zoologist to give an objective description of the cat in his work *Tierleben*. In the 19th century he wrote 'Everything points to the fact that cats fully deserve the friendship of men, and that it is finally time that people become

The witch in the fairy story Hansel and Gretel is always accompanied by cats, her familiars

*Woodcut by
Gustave
Doré of
Puss-in-
Boots, the
hero of
Charles
Perrault's
fairy tale*

aware of the truth and change their unfair and unpopular opinion of these animals.'

This positive attitude towards cats was first reflected in fairy tale literature. By 1697 Charles Perrault had written *Le Maître Chat ou le Chat Botté*, the well-known story of Puss-in-Boots. Perrault included the story in his anthology *Contes de ma Mère l'Oye* which was translated into English in 1729 as *Tales of Mother Goose* and into German in 1812 as *Das Märchen vom gestieftelten Kater*. This was included in the collection of stories made by the brothers Grimm, known as *Grimm's Fairy Tales*. On it Ludwig Tieck based his satirical come-dy *Puss-in-Boots*, a jolly play which critics described as 'poetry for a stag or hen night'. The story of Dick Whittington – three times Lord Mayor of London – and his cat has become equally famous. Since it was first published in 1641, Dick Whittington and Puss-in-Boots have been among the most popular cat stories.

Another favourite subject in the 19th century were tales which the cat purported to write about itself. This genre began with the story of Madame Blasson, *Histoire d'une chatte écrite par elle-même and éditée par XXX*, a tale in which the cat-author told the story of her life.

The first epic character-cat to enter the German literary stage was E. T. A. Hoffmann's celebrated character *Kater Murr* ('Murr the Tom Cat'). Living with his master Abraham, Murr the tom cat is a writer and poet and besides his memoirs he is also described as having written 'serious' works such as *Thoughts and Awareness or Cat and Dog* and *Mousetraps and their Influence on the Beliefs and Energy of Cats*.

There were also some literary cats writing in the anthology *The Public and Family Life of Animals* by Grandville: *The Heartache of an English Cat*, and in another volume *The Heartache of a French Cat*.

Hermann Schiff continued the career of Murr the tom cat with his book *Nachlaß des Kater Murr* ('The Unpublished work of Murr the Tom Cat') which were the 'unknown' adventures of Murr the tom cat.

In *Goethe's Cat* by the Danish writer Sven Leopold, the main character is a kind of keyhole journalist who reports on his master. In the tradition of Murr and Hidigeigei are *Der Trompeter von Säckingen* ('The Trumpeter of Säckingen') by Victor von Scheffels, in which the cat is dressed in the latest Paris fashion, or Carlo the tom cat, the 'Supercat' and main character in a book by Johann Richard zur Megedes. Carlo the tom cat is not only Italian, a diplomat and a hotel cat, but also a follower of Nietzsche, an anti-moralist and an ethical anarchist: a sophisticate among literary cats. While Murr travels by coach through Germany and Hidigeigei takes the train to Paris, Carlo travels only first-class and even crosses the Mediterranean.

In *Pembroke's Cat* by Philip J. Davis, the subject of the literary cat is continued. In it the cat Thomas Gray is a learned university philosopher who astonishes the scholars of Pembroke College, Cambridge.

In Rita Mae Brown's *Pity*

that You are not Dead and *Peace has been Broken*, Mrs Murphy the tiger cats takes on criminal cases and solves the crimes.

Equally clever was 'Francis', the hero of *Felidae I* and *Felidae II* by Akif Pirinçci whose adventures were filmed. In addition, Francis was also the commentator in the *Great Felidae Cat Book* written by Pirinçci and Rolf Degen.

The cat is probably also the favourite animal of poets – indeed cats are mentioned in many poems, appearing by turns lovable, malicious, beloved and predatory. Such poems include *Pangur Ban* by an unknown Irish monk, Martin Opitz's *Auf der Petrarchae Katze*, Heinrich Heine's

Mimi, Friedrich Hebbeil's *Aus der Kindheit* ('From Childhood'), Edouard Mörikes *Die Kutzen Weissling and Sauberschwanz heben an* ('Weissling and Sauberschwanz begin to speak'), Charles Baudelaire's *Les Chats* and Paul Verlaine's *Les Chats*, Gunnar Ekelöf's *Roman Nights*, Jorge Guillen's *Cats in Rome*, Miguel Angel Asturias' *The Cats of Venice*, Pablo Neruda's *Cat's Dream*. and numerous other poems.

Thomas Gray wrote a fine poem *Ode on the Death of a Favourite Cat* and John Keats also sang the praises of cats, though not so widely as T. S. Eliot whose cat poems were published as *Old Possum's Book of Practical Cats*. It was this collection of poems

The Technique *by Pablo Picasso (1962)*

Ernst Kirchner (1880–1938) was another artist who liked to paint cats, as in this painting of the graphic artist Paul Klee

which provided the basis for Andrew Lloyd Webber's hugely successful long-running musical *Cats*.

There were some eerie elements in Theodor Storm's *Bulemann's House* in which tom cats Graps and Schnores are the companions of the misanthropic Herr Bulemann. The yellow cat and the black cat are the only creatures whom he allows near him. When his sister asks him for help for her sick child, he refuses, whereupon she puts a curse on him. This curse is carried out by Bulemann's two cats which grow to the size of tigers and hold their master prisoner in his own house.

The cat in Edgar Allan Poe's *The Black Cat* is equally blood-curdling. Under the influence of alcohol the animal-loving narrator turns into the torturer and tormentor of his beloved black cat. Having hanged it and almost forgotten it, he encounters another black cat, surprisingly similar to his own, whose chest fur became increasingly white with time and takes on the shape of gallows. Faced with this constant reminder and driven by anger and rage, the narrator tries to kill the cat but instead he kills his wife. He bricks up her body in the cellar. Meanwhile the cat has mysteriously disappeared.

The police had become suspicious but in high spirits he takes them round his house, boasting about the excellent quality of the building. To demonstrate this, he taps on the new brick wall whereupon a long, piercing scream is heard. The police tear down the wall, find the corpse and, on its head – the black cat. There are several film adaptations of this famous story.

Equally terrifying is Bram Stoker's short story *The Squaw*, in which a cat takes revenge on the murderer of her young. The murderer is a loud American tourist who foolishly allows himself to be locked up for fun in an 'iron maiden', a box containing spikes used to torture heretics. The lid is held open by a rope held by an attendant. Suddenly the mother of the kittens appears out of nowhere, leaps onto the attendant and scratches his face. This causes him to let go of the string so that the lid falls down, spiking the occupant to death.

Cats are still linked to eerie, strange events in contemporary literature such as the occult thriller *Schrödinger's Cat* by Robert Anton Wilson. Equally creepy are some of the stories of Stephen King, in one of which a zombie cat spreads terror around it. The story was made into a film, as were three other Stephen King short stories in *Cat's Eye*.

Other films with a cat theme include *The Cat Creature*, a horror story in which a mummy comes back to life in the form of a house cat; and *Cat People*, in which people turn into dangerous predators while making love.

The cat in the entertaining film *Bell, Book and Candle* is more mysterious than horrifying. In the film the cat helps her mistress Kim Novak to seduce the innocent James Stewart. In the children's film 'The Cat Prince', two children search a gloomy castle to find their cats killed by an evil man. In order to bring them back to life they must go to fairy-land.

The cat in *Spiegel, das Kätzen* ('Spiegel the Kitten'), a story from the collected novellas by Gottfried Keller, is more delightful and fantastic. Spiegel influences people but

The heroine of Alice in Wonderland *playing with her pet cat Diana. Illustration by John Tenniel, 1872*

in an amusing, cheerful way. The kitten is obliged to sell itself to a magician because of circumstances. The little kitten succeeds in outwitting the magician and manages to be released from its agreement with its owner.

attract the attention and love of people, in the tale entitled *The Cat That Walked by Himself*. 'He walked by himself and all places were alike to him.'

In *Particularly Cats*, the contemporary author Doris

detective stories whose titles always starts with the words *The Cat Who…*, the Siamese cat detectives, Koko and Yum Yum, are extremely intuitive and clever. Last but not least are the numerous cat stories by Lydia Adamson, the pseudonym of a famous writer who herself was an enthusiastic cat lover and cat owner.

The list of essays, novels and stories about cats is endless, while the roster of children's books and picture books about cats is even longer. Also to be mentioned are cartoon films such as Walt Disney's wonderful *Aristocats* and the Tom and Jerry films in which Tom, the cat, is always outwitted by Jerry, the mouse, not forgetting Sylvester, the cat which never succeeds in catching the canary Tweety. Last but not least is the laziest and greediest of cats, Garfield, whose favourite food is lasagne.

It is the fascinating nature of cats which explains why they play such a significant part in literature and the cinema.

The cats in the cat stories by the French writer Colette are also very lovable. She also wrote the libretto for Maurice Ravel's *L'Enfant et les Sortilèges* in which a pair of Siamese cats are given some very funny parts.

On the other hand, the famous Cheshire cat in Lewis Carroll's *Alice in Wonderland* (later made into an animated cartoon film by Walt Disney) is particularly intelligent and subtle. In the *Just-So Stories*, Rudyard Kipling describes how these shrewd animals

Lessing describes without any sentimentality how cats interact with each other and how they interact with people.

Tad Williams also writes about cats in *Dream Chaser and Gold Paw*, as does Joy Smith Aiken in *Solo's Journey*, Cleveland Amory in *The Cats who came for Christmas* and *The Cat Called Polar Bear*. In Jörg Ritter's *The Cat Star*, the cat's famous 'sixth sense' stands the trio Frederic, Castro and Ringo in good stead in their fight against evil. In Lilian Jackson Braun's cat

Having studied cats in the past and present, it is also worth looking at cats in the future, because cats have also invaded science fiction. For instance there is a work by Robert A. Heinlein called *The Cat who Walks through Walls*, in which a cat with supernatural powers inadvertently lands on earth in a spacecraft, causing all security officials to be put on stand-by and ultimately outwitting his followers with clever tricks.

How to look after

cats properly

Every cat has its own territory, whether it lives in a flat, a house with a garden or on a farm. If the cat spends much time roaming around, in the case of a neutered cat this territory can extend to 2 or 3 hectares (5 to 8 acres) which it inspects regularly. If a cat lives exclusively in the home, its territory becomes reduced to the size of its home, which becomes its domain and is claimed as such by the cat.

Even though a cat would normally categorise the other animal occupants of the house as enemies, as prey or, in the case of other cats, as rivals, other house pets are usually accepted without problem. Even a hamster, a mouse or a canary or budgerigar will be readily accepted by the cat as house companions if the new arrival is patiently introduced slowly and the smaller animals are kept in their own surroundings such as a closed cage.

Even cats and dogs may be good friends

Nor is there likely to be a problem if there are dogs in the home because, although cats need their own territory, they also allow the other animals in the house to have their own territory. Any initial enmity soon turns into indifference and cats will quickly ignore the other animals in the house. Sometimes cats may even develop a real friendship with dogs, especially younger animals. Kittens love playing with the

dog of the house. Older cats will at first regard the dog of the house as an enemy, which is why spatial separation of the two animals is advised in the early days. With time, the cat's curiosity will develop and the cat will slowly become interested in the dog. Even though the adult cat and a dog which was already in the home may not become firm friends, they will respect each other. They may sometimes tease each other but on the whole they will keep out of each other's way.

But there will be more serious problems with other cats because they will fight over territory. The new cat will feel uneasy because it will smell that the home territory has already been claimed by other cats as their own. The older cat feels equally uneasy: it sees the new arrival as an intruder and reacts in a negative manner, behaving aggressively, jealously or in an offended manner. In such a case there are no immediate solutions to achieve harmonious co-habitation. The people in the house must step in and help. The new cat should

A cat has its own territory which it will defend if necessary, but it is also prepared to share it with a friend

Right: Cats and dogs also get on very well, although there can be a little play-fighting now and again

Cats and children can become firm friends and have a lot of fun together

be slowly introduced into the territory of the old cat. At first it may not be possible at all to bring them together, so that a brief separation of the two cats may be the best solution. Here too, curiosity will overcome both cats in the end; at first this may take the form of fighting, which will not damage the animals in any way even if the fighting looks rather rough. Very soon they will merely size each other up, calm down and gradually become accustomed to the presence of the other cat. They will then be prepared to share their territory.

Children are particularly fascinated by kittens because they are so charmingly toy-like

Cats and Children

Young cats make very lively, enthusiastic playmates for

small children – but the children must be aware that they cannot play with a cat as if it was a toy. A little over-enthusiastic playing and cuddling of the kitten will not harm it as long as it is not hit or caused any pain. Any sound

of distress by the animal should always be taken as sign to stop, leaving the animal alone and giving it some space. If the cat hisses, shows its claws or meows loudly, the animal should be released immediately to avoid either the child or the animal getting hurt. The child could be scratched or bitten by the kitten if the playing gets too rough. Also excessive, violent embracing and display of affection can frighten the kitten which will be marked by this unpleasant experience for a long time.

It is vital to be careful with babies and cats. Animals will always search the warmth and closeness of their companion – whether another animal or a baby – and this can have fatal consequences for the baby because of the weight of the cat, especially if

the cat sits on the body or head of the baby which is unable to push the cat off. Cats and babies should therefore never be left together without supervision. .

The decision to buy a cat

Before deciding to buy a cat, whether an ordinary moggy or a pedigree cat, it is a good idea first to have you and your family tested for any possible animal allergies. These allergy tests can be carried out any general practitioner.

It is important to find this out because an allergic reaction to cat hair should not be underestimated. It should not be ignored on the basis that itchy eyes and skin irritation do not really matter. If you should notice these negative physical reactions you would be faced with the problem of having to get rid of the newly acquired animal which will already be very much loved. In addition, finding a good home for the cat is often much harder than buying the cat in the first place, particularly when it is a large, adult animal.

Pregnant women should not come into contact with cat's excreta because of the danger of toxoplasmosis, especially during the first pregnancy. The cat will show no sign of suffering from the disease but humans can suffer slight nausea or a light cold. But there is the risk that the baby in the womb could be seriously damaged by it; brain damage and a damaged retina are possble results if the mother suffers from toxoplasmosis during pregnancy. This does not mean that a pregnant woman has to get rid of a cat that is already part of the houshehold, but she should not be the one to clean out the litter tray, since toxoplasmosis is passed on through the excrement of an infected cat. It is also possible to have your cat tested to check whether it is infected, and the pregnant woman can have a blood test to check whether if she has already been in contact with toxoplasmosis. If she has, there is no danger to the unborn baby.

Having established that you and your family are not allergic to cats, you can start thinking about the responsibilities of having a house pet. It is true that a cat is not very demanding: it is easy to look after and does not need spe-

cial care. However, it is important to make sure that the home and furniture meet the requirements and needs of a cat. Even though the new pet will quickly be trained not to scratch the furniture and carpets, some scratches on the furniture must be expected in the first few weeks.

You must also make sure that someone will be able to

The decision whether or not to buy a cat must be taken very seriously and the pros and cons carefully considered

Overleaf: These kittens are quite irresistible; long-haired breeds are particularly beautiful and elegant, but their grooming is more time consuming

look after the cat when you and your family go away on holiday. Cat owners often experience a moral conflict when planning their holiday. On the one hand, putting their beloved cat in a cattery is not always such an unpleasant experience for the cat, since many cattery

Long-haired cats require more care than the ordinary short-haired domestic cat

owners take great care of their charges. So the cat does not take it as rejection. But such professional catteries are obviously quite expensive.

On the other hand, you may not want your cat to have to become accustomed to new surroundings, to new, strange people and to lots of animals. You may also worry about the possibility of infections caught from other animals in the cattery.

An ideal solution is if you know someone who will be happy to come in every day

for a few minutes to look after your cat at home, feeding it and cleaning the litter tray while you are away. Or they may be able to take your cat into their own home.

So if you know you can make arrangements for the cat while you are away, either in a cattery, or with a friend who will look after it, you are ready to buy your cat.

If you are really keen about cats but have no garden or facility to let the cat out for fresh air and regular exercise, don't give up! Millions of cats spend their entire life without ever going out of doors

and they are quite happy like this if they have been accustomed to this kind of life from the very beginning.

Whether you prefer an ordinary, loving, robust child-friendly, cuddly cat or a pedigree cat depends entirely on your individual taste. The

list of pedigree cats and breeds at the back of this book will give you extensive information about the temperament of each breed and the particular attention it may need.

There is no need to elaborate here on the different temperaments of male and female cats, because these only exist in animals which have not been neutered or spayed. Cats can reproduce at a prodigious rate, so whether male or female, your cat should be neutered or spayed because there are already far too many cats which cannot

find a home. These have to spend their life in animal shelters or, more commonly, they have to fend for themselves in the wild. Sadly, far too many animals are abandoned when they stand in the way of their owners' lifestyle.

A cat can sometimes
be acquired by chance –
on a farm for instance

**How to
look after
cats
properly**

In search of a suitable cat

It is possible you may find an abandoned kitten in the street which conquers your heart and which you wish to 'adopt'. But make sure it does not already belong to someone and has just got lost. Otherwise there arc four possibilities for acquiring or buying a cat.

You can obtain all kinds of cat, of every breed, colour and size from private sources. Adult cats in particular are often advertised in classified advertisements and notices in shop windows and supermarkets. Such a cat may be available because the owner no longer wants to keep it, for reasons such as moving house, cat allergy or declining interest. These adult cats usually find it very difficult to acquire a new home because most people want a sweet little kitten when they decide to buy a cat. In fact kittens too are available from private sources, because not

all cats neutered or spayed. In farms especially, cats are often left to procreate naturally and their owners are only too happy to hand them over to cat lovers who are searching for a kitten.

Of course cats are also bred and sold commercially. Pet shops offer both ordinary and pedigree cats while specialised breeders sell the litters of their pedigree cats. Serious breeders take great care of their animals, making sure they are healthy and that their needs are met. If

you are not happy with the way a breeder looks after the cats – for instance, because the animals are kept in cramped quarters – take your leave and look for another breeder whom you approve of, where the animals are looked after with loving care. You can find the addresses of breeders in your area from breeders' societies.

It is best to steer clear of cats which are kept in small,

A cat acquired from a cat shelter will really enjoy its new home, where it will be surrounded by love

Kittens are particularly popular and therefore always find a home much more quickly than older cats

Animal welfare societies are always looking for people willing to take in and care for abandoned house cats

unhygienic cages in ill-run pet shops, because any damage resulting from this lack of care and hygiene will only become apparent later. It is even possible that the kitten is already ill, that it will be

impossible to house-train, or that it will be shy and nervous or aggressive and unapproachable. Make sure the pet shop is run properly, with are orderly, hygienic surroundings. Because of the limited space and the number of animals, cats in a pet shop may not have enough exercise and all their needs cannot be properly met. But fortunately most animals do not spend very long in on display in the cages. Find out how long the animal has been in the shop; ideally a cat should not have been there longer than a week. But remember too that the older and neglected animal will

have more difficulty finding a home; it may be weaker and on the face of it less sweet, but with proper care all this can change. A pet is not just a beautiful object, a new piece of furniture or a toy – these older or neglected cats urgently need a good home and loving care.

An increasing number of cats are abandoned and taken in by animal shelters, especially during the holidays. Many of these cat were bought as tiny kittens but when they no longer look like cuddly toys because of their increasing age and size, they lose their appeal in the eyes of their owners. They

This cat is looking longingly into the distance and dreaming of freedom

will either be abandoned or taken to an animal shelter. When choosing the right kind of animal in an animal shelter, remember that young animals get used to their new surroundings and new people much more quickly and that they are much more trusting than adult cats. But even adult cats do not remain shy

happy that all these requirements have been met, you can make a decision.

As well as the price of certain breeds which depends on the pedigree and the 'demand', you should also take into consideration the cost of future vaccinations and possible medical treatment by the veterinary sur-

be acquired from an animal shelter for a much smaller sum or a donation. Cats are not given away free since this might attract irresponsible people who would not take care of them properly. It is hoped that the need to pay makes people think seriously before taking on the responsibility of a cat. The money is used to pay for vaccinations and the spaying or neutering of the cats.

forever and they do not always have problems in getting used to their new home. That is why you should always take your time when visiting a cat home. Check whether the animal you have chosen is aggressive, whether it allows itself to be stroked and whether it lets you approach it. Check that the surroundings are clean but not too sterile and the the cat's fur looks well-groomed and healthy. When you are

geon. For the animal's health, it is essential to ask for its vaccination certificate of the cat.

Pure pedigree cats are sold by breeders for £100 or more, while pedigree cats bred for exhibition and competition may cost several times that amount. They should be accompanied by a pedigree registration certificate with details of its ancestry for at least four generations.

An ordinary house cat can

Some animal shelters take great care of the animal and do much to ensure their well-being – they are kept in good conditions and live in large groups in well-equipped enclosed areas. Because committed workers in animal shelters only have a limited amount of time and are unable to take in all abandoned cats, it is always worth enquiring from the local cat shelter whether a kitten is available

The prevention of diseases and unwanted kittens

Vaccination, neutering and spaying

Regular vaccination

Cats should be be vaccinated against several life-threatening infectious diseases. These include respiratory viral infections, commonly known as cat flu, an often fatal infectious disease when not treated immediately with antibiotics. The cat should also be vaccinated the feline leukemia virus (FeLV), a very dangerous viral infection, and feline infectious enteritis (FIE). (Vaccination against rabies is not necessary in Great Britain, but it is required when travelling abroad.) This immunistion protection against the most dangerous diseases must be repeated regularly every year.

In addition, cats must be wormed when they reach the age of 12 weeks. Thereafter, they must be wormed every year to prevent them getting tape-worms and eel-worms.

Treatment is usually in the form of tablets added to the food or paste. The paste comes in a little plastic tube and it is very easy to administer: open the cat's mouth a little, taking care not to hurt the animal and squeeze the paste into the mouth. The cat will probably struggle a little because it does not like the taste but it will swallow the paste and lick the rest of it from its mouth.

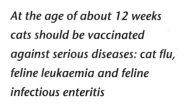

At the age of about 12 weeks cats should be vaccinated against serious diseases: cat flu, feline leukaemia and feline infectious enteritis

Neutering and spaying cats

However cute kittens may be and however natural it is to

have kittens, there are hundreds of thousands of cats which cannot find a home, and the number is still increasing. Often cat owners cannot find homes for their cat's offspring and the fate of unwanted kittens is dark.

This is why it is strongly recommend to spay the female cat and also to neuter the male cat so that it does not mate with unspayed female cats in the neighbourhood, which would then produce unwanted litters. Also, tom cats will become more affectionate, more cuddly and less aggressive. Best of all, they will no longer spray to mark their territory, the function of excretion of sex scent which causes a particularly unpleasant odour.

Spayed cats no longer come into oestrus (that is, sexually receptive). Normally this first occurs when the female

reaches sexual maturity, at the age of four to six months, and it lasts for about ten days. It is a very demanding time for the owner: the cat becomes very nervous, it remains outdoors all the time to try and find a tom cat to mate with, and it rubs itself against every object in the

home. After a few days, the cat signals its readiness to mate by a loud caterwauling and howling which is very nerve-wracking for anyone within earshot. The cat rolls about on the ground and only the heartless would fail to feel sorry for the poor creature. During the period of sexual receptivity the cat will roam outside and it will hardly ever be seen in the house.

Spaying is the only way to spare yourself and your cat this harrowing experience, and the male equivalent is neutering. Both operations take place under full anaesthetic, consisting of removing the female cat's ovaries or the tom cat's testicles. The operation in both cases is irreversible, and it removes all risk of unwanted litters since the animals remain

People who are happy to look after a large number of cats may decide not to have their cats spayed or neutered

But anyone who would prefer to look after just one cat, such as this sweet little kitten, should have it spayed or neutered at the age of about six months

In the southern countries of Europe cats live mostly in the open and congregate near houses where they know they will find food

sterile for the whole of the rest of their life.

Because of the great change in hormone levels caused by the removal of their reproductive organs, the behaviour of a neutered or spayed cat will change drastically. Owners of tom cats will notice this in particular because of the cat will no longer spray to mark its territory and the time-consuming removal of the unpleasant smells will no longer be necessary.

So it is recommended that owners who do not wish to become breeders should have their cat neutered or spayed by the veterinary surgeon when it reaches sexual maturity. The owner will benefit

from a more affectionate, less aggressive pet, while avoiding the risk of contributing to the irresponsible increase of the unwanted cat population.

Sterilisation is an alternative to spaying or neutering; it is less reliable but it is possible to reverse it. In the operation the fallopian tubes are cut or clamped; in the latter case pregnancy is unlikely as a result but not impossible. The severing of the Fallopian tubes or the removal of the womb are reliable methods of contraception but they do not change the instinctual or sexual life of the cat or its behaviour during the period of sexual receptivity. For this

Cats will become noticeably quieter and more affectionate after being neutered or spayed. The oestrus of female cats ceases and tom cats stop spraying to mark their territory

reason sterilisation is now rarely used.

Because all these operations (sterilisation, spaying and neutering) are carried out under general anaesthetic, it is important that the animal should be prepared in advance. In order to reduce the risks of the operation as much as possible, the cat should not be fed on the evening and morning before it. The veterinary surgery carrying out the procedure will give specific instructions.

After the operation the cat must be allowed to recover in peace and quiet, preferably in a room where the animal cannot hurt as it recovers, since at first it will be dazed and staggering. All the cat needs in the room is a comfortable blanket on the floor or in a basket. After the cat has woken up completely, you must make sure that it does not scratch away at the bandage or lick the itchy wound. Even when the cat has recovered from the trauma of the operation – which could be a few hours or the day after the operation – it is important that you try and prevent it from jumping and running around during the few days after the operation. The wound and scar might stretch and open up again. The sutures or stitches will be removed by the veterinary

A cat will be a little tired after its operation but it will recover quickly and will soon be its own lively self again

surgeon about a week later, and tthen he operation will be a thing of the past.

If you want to consider the possibility of your cat producing a litter in the future but do not want this to happen immediately, it is possible to use drug based methods of birth control. These contraceptive drugs are available from the veterinary surgery and they come in the form of tablets or sprays. They will temporarily suppress the sexual receptiveness and fertility of the animal. Anyone who opts for this method of contraception must be aware that to be effective these contraceptive drugs must be administered regularly and punctually. It is a relatively expensive method.

Where and how your cat will live most comfortable in your home

The cat's kingdom

Cats love to snuggle on a warm bed

In an ideal situation cats should live in a cosy, warm home, well-cared for and loved by their owners, and able to go out whenever they like. In order to reduce the

dangers facing the cats when they go outside, there should ideally be very no traffic, a large garden, and meadows and fields.

They also love to snuggle up against each other on a cosy armchair or sofa

Unfortunately, very few cat lovers have a detached house set in a large garden, surrounded by fields and woodland. City dwellers love cats too and it has become quite common for cats to live in flats where they can never to go outside. When you look at the living space in your home, you might decide that it is not large enough and therefore not suitable for a cat. But this is unlikely to be the case, since while a single room is not

enough, the amount of space needed is not enormous, and it will probably have some interesting places to explore which is one of the things a cat needs.

In any case, the outside world is full of dangers for a pet. As well as the traffic which can have fatal consequences for a cat, there may be barbed wire, rat poison in a neighbour's cellar, a dangerous dog across the road, an animal-hating neighbour, or even the professional animal-collector; all of these can pose serious threats to the life

and the freedom of your cat. Consequently there are some owners who love their cats very much and who want to protect them from every possible danger. They will not let them go out, because they would feel terrible if anything happened to their beloved pet.

A gainst this opinion that a cat should never go out for safety reasons, there is a completely different point of view: one that holds that the cat should be able to go outside and satisfy its natural instincts for hunting and exploration.

Individual cat owners will have to decide for themselves what is best for their cat.

It is in fact true that cats which have been accustomed from birth to live in an apartment and never go out are just as happy as those which are able to go out in a garden or to roam around the countryside. So people who live in an flat which makes it impossible for a cat to go out need not feel that they are being cruel to their pet. At the same time, people who live in a house where the cat can go out should weigh up the pros and cons between the cat's freedom to go out and its safety.

There are several things to watch out for if your cat is free to go out. These points are covered in the section *Special tips for special situations*.

The cat's home

Before getting a cat you must be confident that your home is large enough for another inhabitant, because the cat will need a little space to run around. You should not even consider getting a cat if you live in a single room or if you will only allow the cat into one room of the flat. This may seem obvious but there are many people who believe that a cat will happy to live in just a single room only. It will not!

The amount of space a cat needs is access to at least two rooms so that it can roam around a little and explore. You cannot stop a cat from going into the sitting room and lying on the sofa where it can curl up comfortably while its owners are in the room: the

room in which the owners themselves spend a lot of time must not be taboo to the cat.

This is where the problems may start: the newly arrived kitten is not yet used to its surroundings and it will inspect everything from the wardrobe to the sofa and the armchairs. Neither does it yet-know that the armchair is not a scratching pole and that it must not sharpen its claws on the most valuable furniture. You will need a lot of patience and perseverance to train the cat not to scratch the furniture and armchairs. It is possible and indeed strongly recommended to take preventative measures to avoid the

A shoe makes a perfect pillow for a cat – or it will chew it like a bone!

Cats also adore wardrobes and linen cupboards because they are very warm and comfortable with many corners to explore

carpets and furniture being damaged, because prevention is much better than having to carry out difficult or expensive repairs. If you don't, you may feel the only solution is to get rid of your newly acquired pet because it is causing so much damage by scratching.

When acquiring a cat, you also need to buy a litter tray, a scratching pole, a scratching mat and a basket – although most cats will prefer to sleep on your sofa, bed or upholstered chair. You – or rather your cat – will also need a food bowl, a water bowl and a little corner in the kitchen where it can eat in peace. A cat often likes to drag its food out of the bowl and eat it on the floor, so it is a good idea to put the food bowl on a tray or on newspaper. This will make it easier for you to keep the cat's eating corner clean without having to wash it every day. Before deciding where to put the litter tray, you must make sure it is a suitable place where the cat can use it in peace and you are not bothered by the strong smells. Many cat owners put the litter tray in the bathroom because the cat can use the tray without being disturbed and the smell is less of a nuisance. Litter trays are sold in pet shops and some supermarkets. It consists of a rectangular plastic tray which is also available with a top.

This plastic box or tray is then filled with cat litter to a depth of a few centimetres (an inch or so) in which the cat buries its excrement, behaviour which comes naturally to a cat. This also helps to reduce the smell. Various kinds of litter are available in supermarkets. The differences lie in the degree of absorbency, deodorising properties and the ability to form lumps. The best kind of litter is the dark lump-forming kind in which individual lumps can be removed separately with a litter scoop and then topped up with more litter. As a result, the litter tray is always clean and the contents need not be changed every day as would be necessary with litter that does not form lumps. (Incidentally, never throw the soiled litter in the lavatory because it is liable to block the drains!)

Sand, scraps of paper and sawdust are unsuitable for a cat's litter tray because they are unhygienic. This is because they do not absorb strong smells and are not absorbent enough. In addition, the damp paper or saw-dust sticks to the cat's feet and is distributed all over the flat or house.

How often the litter should be changed depends on the habits of the individual cat. Animals which go out a lot will use the tray much less often than a cat which never goes out. Make sure that your cat can use its tray without getting its paws dirty and that it is always free of smells.

A scratching pole is an absolutely necessity for protecting your furniture. There are several types. Scratching poles which are used only for sharpening claws are inexpensive and do not take up much

The cat litter tray should always be kept clean, or this proverbially clean animal will refuse to use it and will find some unsuitable corner instead

space. But because they are not very tall, they are not good for climbing. If you have enough space, it is worth investing in a large scratching pole which can also be climbed, because cats are natural climbers. They adore climbing trees and jumping on walls, and they love to observe their surroundings from a raised position such as a shelf or the top of a cupboard, often to the owner's irritation. A tall scratching pole provides an outlet for this instinct.

You can also make such a scratching pole yourself. All you will need are a pole, some sisal to wind round the pole and some remnants of old carpet to stick on the horizontal surfaces. Instead of a wooden post, a sturdy cardboard tube such as is used at the centre of a roll of carpet can be turned into a scratching poll. Such cardboard tubes are usually obtainable for nothing from carpet shops. They have the further advantage of being up to five metres (16 feet) long and they are easy to cut to size. A cat will be able to stretch out fully on such a tall scratching pole and sharpen its front claws to its heart's content. It will also be able to climb up and jump down without danger. But make sure it is fixed so that it feels secure and solid because a cat will ignore it if it is shaky. You can

also attach toys to the scratching pole such as corks and paper balls on string which it can pull to and fro, as cats love to do.

You should always have a little grass in the house or flat because a cat's stomach needs it to bring up the hairs it has swallowed. These hairs form indigestible hair-balls which

A tall scratching pole is ideal for a cat because it will allow it to use its climbing skills

the cat's stomach is unable to break down. The solution is to let the cat eat grass which will activate the vomiting process. Cats which do not go out have no chance of finding grass, which is why it should be provided indoors. An alternative is to buy special ready-prepared couch grass seeds which only need to be

watered. Another solution is to buy a cypress grass plant which is a beautiful house plant, easy to look after, a vigorous grower and much loved by cats. This will protect your other plants and your cat's health, because some house-plants contain poisonous substances which may damage the cat's health by causing digestive or other serious problems.

Varieties of house plants containing substances poisonous to cats include philodendron, primrose, azalea, poinsettia, crown of thorns, croton, ivy and oleander. You need not get rid of these plants but watch out to see that your cat does not nibble them. By providing grass for it cat to eat, it will not be tempted by the other house plants.

Accident prevention

If your cat spends night after night exploring the neighbourhood, there is a risk that something will happen to it occasionally. Accidents range from small superficial wounds to deep flesh wounds, broken bones, disappearance or at worst a fatal accident on the road. But accidents also happen in the home. Driven by curiosity and carelessness, cats may be seriously injured or even lose their life indoors as well as out. As the proverb has it, 'Curiosity killed the cat' a reference to the cat's irrepressible urge to explore every corner and object in its surroundings. For instance, an open window may be a kitten's undoing because many cats like to squeeze through openings to escape. They may become stuck in the window or fall out of it, which could have serious consequences. More experienced cats know

that a cooker hob or hot plate can be hot and that a burning candle will singe its whiskers. But the young cat has to learn through its mistakes.

You can spare a pet some of these painful experiences by being careful and taking preventive measures. Simply remove the main causes of accidents, as follows.

Always put away needles, pins, drawing pins, pieces of string and any poisonous

substances such as medicinal drugs or cleaning agents. The latter should never be left within reach of a cat, which may walk in it or lick it.

Make sure that pot plants, bowls and vases are secure so that they cannot fall on top of the cat or break into sharp pieces which could cut it. Do not leave a young kitten alone in the kitchen when you are cooking or while the cooker hob is still hot. With time a

It is very important to make the window safe with wire mesh so that it can be opened without worrying about the cat's safety. Cats may easily be tempted to leap out by the sight of a passing bird and this could have fatal consequences

cat will learn and realise that leaping onto a hot stove would very painful: make clear to that the cooker hob and oven are our of bounds. Once the kitten has felt the heat emanating from the cooker, it will realise the danger. Only inexperienced cats jump on top of a cooker, because they do not yet recognised it as a source of heat which can be dangerous.

When switching on the washing machine and closing the refrigerator, check that the kitten has not crawled inside, driven by its curiosity to explore – because they would mean certain death.

Make all the windows and

Cats love to curl up in a tiny space close to their owners

balconies safe with wire mesh, because even an experienced adult cat may be tempted to leap after a passing bird, which could cause it to lose its balance and crash to the ground.

Mouse traps and rat traps should not be placed in any

Every object is interesting in your cat's eyes and it will be closely inspected. This kitten is wondering whether the cardboard roll is better to play with or to sleep on

area to which cats have access, nor should rat poison be sprinkled where cats may wander.

Toys

Cats love to play with moving objects. If no live mouse is available, the cat will be quite content to play with a table-tennis ball which is not too large, not too heavy, and which flies through the air when the cat 'kicks' it with its paws. Other favourite toys are corks and balls of paper, but there also many cat toys available in pet shops and supermarkets. For instance, there are little mice made of cloth which move on their own, activated by a small motor or a spring, or the traditional squeaky rubber bath toy which cats love. Their imagination knows no bounds when they are playing, but make sure that the toys you have made yourself or bought have no pointed ends or sharp sides, and that they cannot be swallowed by your cat. Cats can become very excited by a ball of wool which they happily chase all over the place – but rewinding the wool will be left to you!

*Right:
The umbrella may suffer a bit
from this kitten's interest,
but never mind!*

*The hanging ball of wool is an
irresistible toy for a cat, providing
plenty of feedback*

*Everything that moves is a toy to a cat, whether it is a ball of
wool or of pape, so long as it rolls about when pushed around*

Hints and tips

for the cat owner

Transport
and settling in

The cat or kitten you have
just acquired must be taken
home in a suitable, safe container in which it will be comfortable. Do not put it in a
dark cardboard box or a travel
bag, because it will need
plenty of fresh air even on a
short journey. Also, a dark
box will be psychologically
very upsetting for the animal.

So, before collecting your

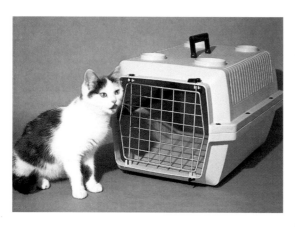

*For
travelling,
your cat
should
always be
put in a
cat carrier.
This may be
plastic, as
above, or
a wicker
basket (top
right) which
can then
double up as
a bed (right)*

new kitten or cat, buy a special cat carrier. These are
made of plastic or wicker, and
they are available from pet
shops and supermarkets at
varioud prices. The door is
made of wire mesh, enabling
the cat to look out, and it can
be securely closed so that the
cat cannot escape during the
journey. This is important
because many cats are frightened by the noise of a car and
the traffic, making them
panic so they try to escape.

Make sure that the carrier is

large enough for the new cat
and that it can be firmly
secured to the back seat of the
car with a safety belt. Otherwise it could roll off if the car
stops suddenly, which could
hurt or seriously injure even a
small, agile animal.

Do not pick up a kitten by
the back of the neck because
this could cause it serious
permanent injury. You may
have seen a cat carrying her
young in this way, and it is
the method often used to

carry rabbits, but you should
never use the technique with
a cat or kitten. A cat should
be picked up with both
hands, one hand supporting
the stomach under the front
legs, and the other the back
legs and bottom. In this way,
the cat is held securely and
cannot get away, and it will
not be able to scratch you
with its claws if it panics.

Sometimes it takes a lot of
patience to persuade a cat to
go into the cat carrier because

many cats do not like being put in a box. But it may be tempted by a delicious morsel of food put at the back of the carrier; sooner or later curiosity and a tasty titbit will attract the cat into the carrier.

As soon as you get home, open all the doors inside the house – but of course none of those leading outside. Put the carrier on the floor and open

the door. The cat will investigate and explore its new home on its own. With luck it will quickly discover the litter tray and the food bowl. Then, driven by curiosity, it will proceed to inspect its new environment carefully, room by room. Let it do this slowly in its own time. Do not force it to go in any particular direction or to sit in a particular place. But show it its litter tray (if it has not

already found it), its eating corner, its scratching pole and its 'bed' or basket. In fact a cat basket may be an unnecessary expense since your cat will decide for itself where it wants to sleep – which will probably be near you.

Here is another tip to avoid later misunderstandings between you and your new pet. If there is a room in the

house or flat where you do not want the cat to go, you must forbid it from entering it at the very start. If it once enters the room it will always believe there is something interesting to find in it and it will do everything possible to get into it again, driven by its innate curiosity. This can be very irritating. However, it is best not to prevent the cat from entering any rooms in which you yourself spend a

lot of time, such as the bedroom. Because the cat will enjoy being near you, it would be hard to keep it out of any room in which you spend a lot of time.

Getting to know your kitten and giving it a name

During the first stages of getting to know each other, you will need to show your kitten a lot of care and attention. It is particularly important to stroke and cuddle it so that it will feel comfortable in its new home, and also to create a feeling of closeness between the two of you.

If you give the kitten a name soon after its arrival and use it often, it may soon even react to it. Cats can never be trained like dogs – they will not come when you call them and they will not obey orders or fetch things. But they are able to recognise

A cat always wants to be near people. This is why it loves to sit on the table when we are sitting round it…

… while this cat is still waiting for an owner who will also let it sit on the table, surrounded by humans

certain signals, including its name if it is a pleasant, melodious sound.

Traditional cat names such as Pussy may be a little boring and old-fashioned, but they are the kind of sound that a cat will react to. Two-syllable words containing the vowels 'i', 'o' and 'a' are at the top of the list of sounds which cats like. Names like Maggie, Charlie, Pussy, Susie, Felix and Josie are therefore excellent. Try and think of a short, harmonious, unusual name! Here are a few suggestions: Humphrey, Didi, Lily, Lady, Jenny, Mimi and Maisie or simply Max.

A few ground rules for training your cat

After your cat has finished exploring its new home and when it has become a little accustomed to you, the difficult process of training must begin. It is widely believed that cats cannot be trained –

some even say that cats must not be trained because it contradictz their very nature. But there are some ground rules which every cat owner will want to follow in the interests of protecting the sofa, the armchairs, the curtains and the carpets.

House-training will be coverede in more detail later. In

Driven by curiosity, the cat inspects and sniffs the food circumspectly. Then it quickly pinches it from under its owner's nose – food tastes so much better when it's shares

fact cats are usually very clean and naturally house-trained if they are not removed too early from their mother. Exceptionally there are 'sick' animals which, completely out of the blue, forget their training and – in the worst scenario – choose your bed as their lavatory.

Experience
and punishment

Like all animals, cats learn from experience. So the training process involves associating an action with something positive, and repeating the operation whenever possible.

In the same way, if a cat experiences something that it finds unpleasant in a particular situation, it will always try and avoid that situation in the future. However, a cat can only learn if the situation or action is *immediately* associated with the consequences. Belated punishment is a complete waste of time because a cat cannot think abstractly as humans do. A cat is unable to associate the scratching of the leather sofa with the subsequent 'beating' or 'punishment' it receives if there is any length of time between the two events.

So the cat should only be rewarded or punished immediately it has done something good or bad. If it has behaved well, reward it with a tasty morsel or a cuddle. If the cat has done something wrong, 'punish' it immediately. But never hit your kitten with a newspaper as dog breeders sometimes recommend for puppies.

The cat must not become aware that it is you who is punishing it. It must believe that the punishment is

directly linked to its behaviour. For instance, you could frighten it a little when it scratches the sofa: a sudden unpleasant noise usually helps to deter the cat from scratching. Some cat experts recommend rattling a chain or lobbing a bunch of keys towards it. Be sure to aim it at the vicinity of the cat, not directly at it! Other techniques include clapping your hands loudly to frighten it, or aiming some water in its direction, using a plant spray (in this case you may exceptionally aim at the cat).

Ideally the cat will soon learn – like Pavlov's dog – that scratching furniture is directly associated with a loud, unpleasant noise or with the water it dislikes, and will in future make a detour to avoid these deterrents. But if the cat knows that you are the source of the noise or the water, it will simply take care to avoid you, while continuing to scratch the furniture. This is the opposite of what you were trying to achieve: your cat avoids you but fails to associate scratching the sofa with anything unpleasant.

Cats are fascinated by shoes. But if you want to keep them smart to wear again later, it's better to keep them in a closed cupboard

The appeal of furniture to cats

A prerequisite for keeping your cat away from furniture is to provide it with a scratching pole which it can use to sharpen its claws and on which it can have a good romp. If you have tried to economise by not buying one you will soon incur other costs, because your cat will use your furniture and carpets as a scratching pole and climbing frame and it will be hard to discourage it from doing so.

If your cat continues to scratch the furniture in spite of the scratching pole and a scratching mat, stop it immediately but gently. The best and only way to do this is to say a firm 'NO' while removing it from the sofa and taking it to the scratching pole. A similar reprimand should stop it from jumping on the table when you are eating. Catch it when it is about to jump, scold it a little and put your hand in front of its face so that it cannot jump. If your cat is already on the table, put it on the floor. In time it will learn that these

places are taboo so far as scratching, sitting and begging is concerned. A small distraction such as a toy can be a helpful way of diverting its attention.

Does the cat recognise its name?

If you would like your cat to recognise its name and also to come when you call it, you should use its name as often as possible so that the animal recognises the connection between its name and itself. This can be very useful if your cat is in the habit of

going out on little expeditions. You should always call your cat in a friendly tone and you must never use its name in connection with anything unpleasant. While your 'No' should be loud and firm, you should pronounce the cat's name affectionately so that it recognises the difference in meaning from the tone of your voice. If you pronounce its name in a sharp manner because it has done something wrong and then proceed to punish him, it will no longer come to you when you call it but rather run away when it hears its name. Praise is an important

Left: These beautiful, elegant creatures prefer to watch the world go by from an elevated position! It is also an ideal place to have a nap

Who is that calling me? Cats usually react very quickly to the sound of their name, as can be seen here from the pricked ears and alert look

part of training your cat. As soon as it comes to you when you call it, you should praise it in an affectionate voice and stroke it a little, so that it knows that it has done well. When it uses his scratching pole instead of the curtains to 'do' its claws, again you should praise it and repeat its name several times in a loving voice.

Taking your cat for a walk – with a collar and lead?

Occasionally you see a cat being walked on a lead by its owner, and indeed the wearing of a lead outdoors is compulsory in some parts of the USA. But how is this possible with an animal which always does what it wants and rarely follows anyone? With some effort it is possible to achieve this because going for a walk on a lead can also be taught and learned.

Some cats love walking in company while others loathe it. For instance, Siamese cats frequently enjoy going for a walk on a lead and other pedigree cats will learn to do so quite easily. But ordinary house cats will seldom follow their owner; they much prefer to be on their own, wandering seemingly aimlessly and exploring the world in their own time.

It is the cat which will determine the speed of the walk and sometimes even indicate the direction. The cat will take a few steps, then stop for a rest. It may lie on the grass and absorb all the new impressions around it. Then it may suddenly leap in one direction to chase a passing insect, then dash off in the opposite direction to avoid an approaching dog.

In order to avoid this kind of problem as much as possible, it is advisable to walk your cat either in the evening or very early in the morning. Cats love the dark, but the traffic noises can be alarming and the other impressions it comes across could prove too

tempting for the cat to investigate. It will probably be more anxious than curious on its first walk and will probably jump up every time a car goes by if you have not taken shelter behind a bush or wall.

In order to minimize your cat's anxiety, choose peaceful itineraries and times when there is very little traffic. But you should remember when you take your cat for walk on a lead that it is not like a dog and will not follow you like a well-trained animal. It will always return to you so that you will have the impression that your cat is following you. But appearances are deceptive: as soon as it realises that is alone outside and sees an

If there is no access to grass outside, you should keep a little grass indoors for your cat. This may be displayed in an elegant container like a house plant

interesting clump of bushes, it will disappear. But there is no need to worry. As soon as the cat has finished exploring the bushes and chasing the mice and insects, it will return to you and continue walking with you. Such a walk with a collar and lead could prove quite difficult, because the lead often becomes tangled in trees and bushes when the cats runs

On a walk the cat will carefully examine and sniff the grass before it decides whether or not it is going to eat it

around and climbs up trees. This can prove too much for some people, but this is normally because they are not sufficiently patient and want to be in charge of the speed and direction of the walk. It has to be admitted that this is impossible because the cat will always have its own agenda and it is very headstrong.

Getting used to a collar and lead

You should only take your cat out for a walk with a collar and lead when it cannot go out on its own for whatever reason. Obviously it is easier for you and for your cat if it can go out on its own.

But every animal should be allowed to get accustomed to a collar and lead. Sooner or later it will prove useful, for instance when going to the veterinary surgeon, moving to a new home and when on holiday. To ensure that the cat does not get hurt or escape on such occasions, it can wear a special cat harness which consists of two straps linked together. The front one goes round the neck and the other round the belly of the cat.

The collar itself should also have a tag bearing the cat's name and the name and address or telephone number of the owner. This collar with a name tag should always worn when the cat goes out on its own so that it is recognized as a domestic pet rather than a stray, and so that it can be returned to you if it does get lost. Choose an elastic collar which is easily opened with a press-stud so that your cat will not be strangled if its collar gets stuck in a bush.

The lead should be at least

3 metres (10 ft) long and it should be attached to the harness, never to the collar. The best leads are the ones which extend and roll up again automatically, because they give the cat the greatest freedom to run around.

When you take your cat for a walk, do not be tempted by the little bell attached to the collar which is intended to warn birds of the approaching cat. It does not help the birds at all and your cat will be forced to put up with its constant tinkling, which will probably be as irritating to you as it is the cat. In any case, healthy birds do not let themselves be caught by cats because even without the bell they notice the cat sneaking up on them long before they are in danger. A cat can only catch sick, weak or injured birds.

A cat harness is much safer than a simple cat collar. The harness should carry a tag with the name and address of the owner on it

like this across the road or to the car. If your kitten gets into a panic or tries to escape, it is pointless to try and restrain it, as it will make clear by digging its claws into your flesh. As soon as you let it go, the cat will probably run away in panic. In such a situation, a cat carrier is absolutely essential for safety.

Travelling with your cat in the car

Unlike people and almost all dogs, cats are not particularly keen on travelling by car. The new surroundings and the many unknown, loud noises make them anxious and even terrified. The cat suddenly realises that it is no longer in its own territory. It has no way of knowing that it will soon be back in its own home.

It is therefore important to get the kitten used to travelling by car very gradually. At first it must be allowed to inspect his new 'room' in its

'Oh no, they want to pick me up again', this kitten seems to be thinking as it hides its face behind its paws

When crossing the road, you must carry the cat without letting it scratch you. But you should not have to force the cat to stay in your arms. Instead you must try and get it used to being held inthis way. This will take a little while and a lot of patience.

It is obviously much easier to train a kitten than an older cat. Pick up the kitten very gently, hold it in your arms and stroke it while you talk to it so that it it feels comfortably in your arms. When the cat has had enough cuddling and stroking, it will jump out of your arms onto the ground. Do not force it to stay in your arms but just let it go. Any constraint on your part will only damage your relationship with the cat. If the cat feels happy and com-

fortable in its owner's arms, it will often come and sit like this of its own accord because it enjoys being cuddled. To prevent the cat escaping, whether in the street or in the veterinary surgery, it is important to pick up the cat in the right way: one hand under the front legs and the other round its back legs and bottom. But until the cat is relaxed being held in this way, it is not safe to carry it

When travelling by car with your cat, you must always put it in a cat carrier, and secure it to the seat with a safety belt

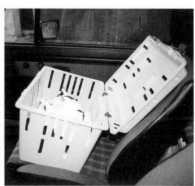

own time before you drive off. As soon as your cat feels secure in the car, you can move on to the next stage: starting the engine. The noise of the engine will make an anxious cat hide, but it will eventually become used to it.

A few cats remain frightened of travelling in the car all their life, although it cannot always be avoided. For example, the veterinary surgery may only be accessible by car and visits to it cannot be avoided, even though you can see the fear in the animal's eyes. Anxious cats will be happiest ravelling in a closed cat carrier – which you should use in the car in any case. Sitting in the carrier, the cat will be shaken about less , safer and therefore more relaxed. In addition, it will not lose its balance and stumble whenever the car starts and stops. The more adventurous cat may prefer to sit on the shelf at the back of the car rather than in the basket, but for safety reasons this must never be allowed. In the event of a car crash the cat – and in the worst scenario you as well – are likely be seriously injured or even killed.

Cats, their habits and routines

Cats love routine. They have a set daily routine and highly accurate body clock which regulates this routine. They spend a large part of the day dozing and sleeping, playing and grooming themselves and only a few hours chasing around, running and exploring the surroundings.

Why do cats suddenly stop being house-trained?

One of the cat's greatest quality is its amazing cleanliness. If your cat urinates or defecates next to the litter tray or, even worse, on the carpet, there is always a good reason. Often it is because the litter tray is very dirty or because the cat is ill. It may also simply be that you have bought the 'wrong' litter or that you have cleaned it with a new cleaning product. If none of these reasons apply, then you should go to the vet and ask for advice. If it is confirmed that there is no physical illness, you must look for some

psychological reason which is the cause of this unusual behaviour. A house cat which is used to people is very sensitive to any change in the behaviour of the people around it, such as the departure a member of the family or the arrival of a new guest, or even worse the arrival of other pets which the cats sees as an invasion of its territory. This temporary blip in the cat's cleanliness should therefore be seen as a reaction to changes in its environment.

However, the most serious problems of house-training occur with cats which have not been spayed or neutered:

Cats often lick their fur to keep themselves clean but when they are a little tired they lie down to wash themselves

Your cat may behave rather strangely when a new one arrives in the house. For instance, a house-trained cat may suddenly have 'accidents'

90% of these will deliberately urinate outside their litter tray in order to mark their territory.

If your cat has only missed once, right next to the litter tray, it could be because it was frightened by something or someone. Do not be too angry with it if it does not happen again. If the site of the incident is in your bed or on the carpet, you must wash the spot very carefully and thoroughly but do not scold the cat, because that will not deal with the reason for its unusual behaviour.

To wash the soiled area, use soap suds or water with some vinegar. This will neutralise the smell and prevent the cat from its natural tendency to use the same place again, because it does not like the smell of vinegar. Another effective method to stop all repetition is to conceal the place, either by putting the litter tray on the spot or by covering it with newspaper or foil. Naturally, you cannot do this with pieces of furniture or the bed. But ordinary bed-linen and loose covers can just be washed in the washing machine. The cat will no longer be able recognise his marking because the smell will have disappeared in the wash.

How could anyone ever be cross with such a sweet little cat?

The aggressive cat

One hears of aggressive cats which are immediately on the defensive if they are approached, however gently, reacting by showing their teeth and their claws. Such an animal will flatten its ears and whiskers, adopt a stalking position and start hissing and snarling. But these are also indications that the cat is about to flee, fear having caused this 'aggressive' panic

attack. Only when the cat sees no way out of its situation will its fear drive him to take on a defensive attitude, which then turns into aggression as with other predators. This aggressive behaviour is often triggered by jealousy – which can directed towards people or any other animals in the house.

Sometimes, however, it is the unfriendly approach by a human which leads to the animal's defensive reaction,

which is then misinterpreted as aggressive. Because a cat is very self-willed, forcing it to do anything will only lead to a defensive reaction: whether picking it up or stroking it against its will, it will react by scratching the uncomprehending person. This can also happen quite suddenly, the contented purring turning unexpectedly to panic. If a cat sees no way out, it will fight, scratch and bite to get away. The reason for this

behaviour is that when the cat has had enough cuddling and cannot see a way out, it will panic and become very aggressive.

Another reason for a cat's apparent aggression is over-excitement. Boredom and a lack of play and exercise can lead to a situation whereby the cat's natural energy builds up to such a level that it suddenly erupts violently. It suddenly starts running through the house or flat as

A cat which looks threatening is probably just being on its guard. It will defend itself if it feels cornered

This frightened, timid little kitten is meowing in distress ...

if possessed, knocking over all kinds of objects, without any regard for the other inhabitants, whether human or animal.

This wild play with any other cat of the household soon turns into a serious fight in spite of them usually being on friendly terms. This behaviour is noticeable in cats which cannot give vent to their natural hunting and playing instincts because they live exclusively indoors, never being allowed to go out. The lack of exercise and play then leads to an uncontrolled outburst of energy in the house.

These violent outbursts of energy and aggressive behaviour also occur in animals which have not been spayed or neutered . In this case, the aggression is triggered by a surge of hormones. Cats also behave like this when they are on heat, but male cats in particular defend their territory against animal and human 'rivals'. The simplest solution is the spaying or neutering of the animal; otherwise you can go to the vet who can help your cat by giving it some hormones, thereby alleviating its 'sexual anguish'.

The nervous kitten

Unpleasant experiences are often the cause of cats feeling uncomfortable in the presence of people, particularly strangers. They may hide as soon as they hear someone approaching. A cat may hide in a cupboard whenever it hears the door bell, not coming out again until the unwelcome guest has left. If, after close examination, the cat recognizes that the visitor will not harm it, it will very cautiously emerge from its hiding place. If the visitor is quiet and not too rough in its movements, the cat may even allow itself to be stroke after a while, striking up a friendship with the visitor. But this will only be if it likes the person: loud footwear, excessive gesturing or loudly

clomping feet will drive the cat away again.

Such shy cats must be treated with great care and patience. One of the biggest mistakes is to drag it out of its hiding place to 'introduce' it to any visitors. This would make it even more anxious. Every forced approach is deemed to failure – the cat will only come out in its own time when it has decided that it is safe.

Reassure the shy little kitten by showing it that it is being left in peace, that you will not force it to do anything it does not want to. Do not make any noise and do not frighten the kitten. Do not force, shock, frighten or hurt it, because that would only drive it even further away. Like this, the kitten will notice that its new environment is quite safe and that you are a very pleasant, quiet companion. After a few days or even weeks, the cat will come out more and more often and even come near you. Gradually it will overcome its fear of the unknown and begin to trust you and the other occupants of the household.

The opposite character is the very outgoing cat: it loves

... or hiding as soon as anyone approaches

Lying on the desk, the cat enjoys some 'education', but what it likes best is being tickled

sleeping on the pillow and will sit on the newspaper just as someone is about to read it. When it goes out of the house, it will follow anyone, allowing them to pick it up and go to their house with them. Whenever a visitor arrives, it will immediately jump on their lap.

Unfortunately for some people, there are also some cats who want more than cuddling, regularly waking up their owners because they want some food or just want to play. The best way of dealing with such clinging cats is simple to ignore their unreasonable demands. As soon as the cat realises that its attempts to wake you up are in vain, it will stop. But you will need a lot of patience. Stay in bed and pretend to be asleep: a sleeping play-mate is no fun! After a few attempts the cat will let you sleep in peace, but you must be consistent and never give in.

More ruthless solutions such as barring the cat from the bedroom, will not necessarily help. It is likely simply to encourage its curiosity and it will still keep you awake for hours with its scratching and meowing.

Short summary of the rules for training cats

If you are very patient and consistent when applying the rules, take into account the interests of the cat, show love and affection, and do not force the rules upon it but introduce them in a playful manner, you will end up with a very pleasant companion. Your furniture too will benefit from it, remaining unmarked by scratches!

But never forget that you are 'training' a cat and not a dog. Remember that a cat cannot be trained in the same way as a dog. A cat will not 'sit' or 'go' when you order it to, but a cat will learn not jump on the table when tell it not to in the right tone of voice.

Many a well-trained cat likes to lie on the table even though it knows very well that it is not allowed to sleep on it or climb on particular items of furniture. As soon as it hears its name in a particular voice, accompanied by the words 'no' and 'down', it will usually jump off the table. The sharp tone of the voice is

often sufficient to make a cat realise that it has done something wrong.

On the other hand, a more timid cat may be more obstinate, sneaking onto the table secretly and avoiding being caught. It does not go there to be told that it must get off the table – it anticipates the 'no' so as not to be addressed in that harsh, unloving tone of voice.

If an owner is very ambitious, with a lot of patience and affection it is possible to teach a healthy cat to perform some tricks. But 'holding out a paw' and 'turning a somersault' are tricks for the performers in a circus. Why should a house cat be trained like a circus artist?

With two cats on the table, there is hardly room to sit reading the newspapers...

Feeding tips for cats

You must ensure that your cat has a well-balanced diet, one which is suited to its digestive system, so that it keeps in good health. This is why you should not feed your cat exclusively on left-overs, even if you have been told that domestic animals can act like a refuse disposal unit. Apart from the fact that cats dislike many of the foods which people like, your cat is not a dustbin. To make sure that your cat has a healthy diet, you should allow an adequate budget of roughly £15 to £20 per month. It is true that it is hard to replicate a cat's natural eating habits at home, but with prepared tinned cat

Cow's milk is not good for adult cats. They should therefore be gradually weaned from it when the time is right

food, you will be able to give your cat an appropriate diet rich in the vitamins it needs.

Cats which hunt for their food will eat mice, rats, small

Every cat needs its own feeding area

rabbits and insects. They devour their prey with its fur, bones and all; the innards, bones and flesh of small rodents are completely swallowed and digested.

This natural diet provides the cat with proteins, fats, carbohydrate, minerals and vitamins – everything that an animal needs to healthy. On the basis of the nutrients found in the cat's natural diet, it is obvious that it needs a diet of meat-based wet food. Plenty of protein, a little fat and some carbohydrate are the basis of a healthy diet for a cat. As well as the right food, you must also provide a bowl of fresh water; an average cat may drink about 200 ml (7 fl oz) daily.

The amount of food eaten depends on the age and the weight of the cat. For adult cats (from the age of seven onwards), the cat should have two meals, morning and evening, always at the same time of the day. Whether fresh or from a tin, the food should be served at room temperature and never hot or directly from the fridge.

A small cat with a body weight of about 2 kg (4½ lbs) needs between 200 and 250 calories a day, while one

weighing 4 kg (9 lbs) needs about 350 calories a day.

Young kittens (up to 8 weeks) are fed up to six times a day, in the 3rd and 4th month, four times a day, and in the next two months, three times a day. Kittens like milk and adult cats do as well, which is unfortunate because their digestive system cannot cope it and they therefore get diarrhoea. So kittens should be weaned from milk by diluting it with increasing amounts of water until it is pure water. If your adult cat still loves milk, now and again you can give it a little bowl of condensed milk.

To be certain that the cat has all the vitamins and nutrients it needs, commercial prepared cat food is best. Even though this may seem a little heartless, the selection and composition of nutrients and vitamins of pre-prepared cat food is versatile and well-balanced.

About 300 g (10 oz) of tinned cat food (so-called wet food) per day is quite enough for a cat of about 4 kg (9 lbs). It is made from fish or meat products with cereals and added minerals. It normally contains about 6–10% protein, 4.5 % fat, 2% minerals and over 80% moisture, and it is enriched with additional vitamins. You should also give the cat some dry food such as cat biscuits, because

A complete cat tray contains three bowls: one for wet food, one for dry food and one for fresh water

this is good for their teeth. If your cat's main meals consist of wet food, do not give it too much dry food because this contains as many calories as wet food.

Naturally, you can give your cat fresh food but it must be well prepared and be suitable for cats in order to meet the animal's nutritional requirements and thus keep healthy. But remember that, if you do give your cat fresh food, raw fish, ham, bacon

and cabbage is not very digestible, nor is food with a lot of added sugar or very spicy foods. As already mentioned, cow's milk gives adult cats diarrhoea and no cat can

This cat is a little on the plump side ...

A little plumpness does noone any harm but overweight cats do suffer because their excessive weight restricts their movements

eat raw potatoes. Cooked fish must have all bones completely removed. Raw pork can cause the fatal Aujeszky's disease (similar to rabies), while raw chicken and eggs can result in salmonella, another very dangerous disease. If the chicken is cooked, remove all the bones very carefully before you give it to your cat because the small ones could easily get stuck in the cat's throat with fatal consequences. To avoid an excess vitamin C (which can lead to bone growths and changes in the joints), do not give your cat more than 1–2 portions of liver per week.

If fed on fresh food, a cat of average size cat should have a varied diet of cooked, unseasoned meat, fish and chicken, amounting to about 150–250 g (5–9 oz) per day, with added cooked cereals and vegetables, for instance about 25 g (1 oz) rice or pasta per day.

Since tinned food is specially produced to satisfy cats' nutritional needs, there is no reason for them any longer suffer from symptoms of dietary deficiency. In fact, many cats are much too fat. Being overweight can harm cats as much as humans: according to research carried out at Cornell University, in the United States, it can lead to diseases like diabetes, as well as causing painful joints, and skin and fur problems.

Tests carried out on 2,000 overweight cats showed that excessively fat cats could no longer reach all their body parts with the tongue and paws, so that they were unable to groom themselves properly; as a result they would suffer health problems after a while.

To improve this situation, an overweight cat, the amount of food served, should be gradually reduced and the cat should also have more exercise. Try and play active games with your overweight cat!

Every cat has its favourite food, but avoid the temptation to give it this all the time. A cat should have a varied diet.

You will soon find out your cat's favourite delicacy, which you can give it to tempt it, praise it or spoil it. This could be anything ranging from vegetables to meat or fish such as crab, salmon, peas, diced or sliced cheese. Some cats adore a small bowl of fromage frais.

Cats will only be able to walk gracefully along thin branches if they are fed with the right kind of food and are not overweight …

Looking after

your cat

When the cat washing itself is not enough

Cats love washing themselves and they do it very conscientiously: they can reach almost all the parts of their body with their rough, moist tongue and they spend hours every day cleaning themselves. The cat's tongue – and you will notice this when it

Two friends clean each other by licking the places they cannot reach themselves with their tongues

Cats can be very affectionate and embrace each other

licks you – is covered with small scale-like protuberances called papillae and is therefore very rough. This makes it easier for the cat to pick up food from the ground and enables them to clean their hair vigorously and thoroughly. The moist, rough tongue also removes all the dirt and dust in the hair. This daily cleaning of their hair also means that cats swallow a lot of hair which they cannot digest. Those parts of the body which they cannot reach with their tongue – such as their face – they clean with their paws. To do this, they first lick their paw to

wet it and then rub their cheeks, eyes and ears vigorously. When two or more cats live together, there is often such a strong bond between them that they lick each other – a wonderful display of friendship and affection which is always a pleasure to see.

However, only shorthaired cats can wash themselves completely. longhaired cats need the help of their owner who must go through their hair with a brush and a comb. But cats which are ill or have fleas or other parasites, and those who are too fat to reach all the parts of their body alsoneed human assistance. If a cat's hair is not cleaned regularly by itself or with a brush it will become matted and thus lose much of its shine and beauty. The cat itself will feels uncomfortable if its hair

is matted. This is why a long-haired cat should be groomed every day for a few minutes with a brush and comb.

Shorthaired cats still need to have their hair checked on a regular basis. If your cat goes out it must be checked regularly for fleas and lice. If it is free of fleas and lice, its hair will still benefit from a weekly brush. Most cats derive great pleasure from being brushed but there are a few who dislike it intensely and resist with all their might. That is why it is advisable to start brushing you cat from an early age – your cat will then be grateful to you for it. If an adult cat refuses to be brushed and combed, try this simple trick: alternate stroking and brushing. The cat will hardly notice the difference or notice the brush or comb. All it will be aware of

is that your hand sometimes feels slightly rougher.

To clean your cat's hair you will need a coarse comb and a wire brush with round-ended bristles. First go slowly and carefully through the hair with the coarse comb, making sure you comb the hair in the right direction to remove knotted and matted hair. These knots and matted hair can easily be removed by pulling the hair apart very gently. If the knots are too difficult to remove, cut them out very carefully using a small pair of scissors.

Then, using the small wire brush with rounded ends, brush the hair in the right direction. This is a part of the operation which the cat enjoys enormously because it feels like a massage on its skin. In addition, brushing gives the hair a beautiful shine. When disentangling the knots, make sure you do it very gently so as not to hurt the cat. You must be particularly careful when brushing the cat's belly because the nipples are very sensitive. It is very important not to hurt the cat because otherwise it will always associate brushing and combing with pain and therefore refuse to be brushed in the future.

Although you must be gentle when brushing and combing the cat, you must also do it thoroughly. If you only

comb through the ends of the hair, you will not catch the knots buried deep down in it. In the course of brushing the cat, you should also look out for parasites. If you notice any bare patches or an unusual loss of hair, take the

cat to the vet because in most cases this is caused by hormonal imbalances, mineral or vitamin deficiencies or by a fungus.

You can also buy special gloves with bobbles which remove loose hair as you stroke the cat. A slightly damp cloth, rubbed over the loose hair will also do the

trick, thus reducing the risk of matted hair. It is particularly important to brush your cat and remove loose hair in autumn and spring when they shed their old hair. This will help your cat by saving it from swallowing large amounts of hair when it grooms itself. These would make hairballs which will have to be vomited up.

A small amount of butter or vegetable oil added to the cat's food will make its hair shiny again. Do not add too much or it may cause diarrhoea. If this happens, you should reduce your cat's fat intake and if necessary remove all fat from the diet.

Should a cat be bathed?

Cats are so clean that a real bath is quite unnecessary.

To prevent a Persian cat's long hair becoming matted and to keep it in good condition, it must be brushed or combed daily.

Infact all cats (apart from Turkish Van cats) will make an enormous detour to avoid the smallest puddle – although ironically they are often fascinated by a dripping water-hose. Your cat will definitely not enjoy a bath or a shower, so it is best avoided unless it is essential.

If the cat has fleas, it is possible to wet the animal very briefly and use a special shampoo. But you can also use powder which is just as effective and saves you the difficult experience of washing and shampooing your cat.

However, sometimes nothing else will help but soap and water: for instance when the hair is so encrusted with dirt that neither the cat's tongue nor the brush can get rid of it.

If you have to bath your cat, fill a small basin or bowl with about 10 cm (4 in) of water between 30 and 35° C (86 to 95° F). Put the cat in the bowl so that it can support itself on the edge of the basin or bowl or place a non-slip rubber bathmat in the basin so that it will not slip. Be careful not to splash water in its ears or eyes. When you

Left: This little kitten licking its front paw is quite irresistible

have finished washing the cat, wrap it in a soft, warmed towel. If your cat does not object, blow-drying is even better. It is very important to dry the cat thoroughly to prevent it from catching cold.

Cleaning the cat's eyes, ears, claws and teeth

Some cat owners believe the best way of saving their furniture from being damaged by the cat is to have their cat's claws clipped. There is some merit in this argument but if the clipping is not done properly, it can cause irreparable damage to the cat, because beyond the tips of the claws are blood vessels and nerve ends which could easily be damaged by inexperienced hands and excessive clipping. As well as the risk of hurting your cat and inflicting serious damage, it is all too easy to remove one of the cat's most important working tools which are used to climb, jump, grab their prey and defend itself if necessary. The cat will make sure that its claws are the sharp and the right length – so long as they have a tree or scratching pole to do it on.

If clipping is necessary – for instance if the cat gets stuck in the carpet with its claws because they have not

been sharpened properly – clipping should only be done by an experienced person, using special clippers. Before you try it yourself, ask the vet to show you how to do it.

Cats hate being examined and cleaned but it has to be done

You will also learn whether and when the process should be carried out.

Ears

The cat's ears need to be checked regularly for cleanliness. If they are dirty with wax and your cat is quite relaxed, the external ear

The cat's teeth will only remain strong and healthy if they are clean. Check them regularly and if you notice any plaque or tartar, take the cat to the vet who will remove it. This will stop the gums from becoming infected, which would make the teeth loose

(only) can be cleaned with a soft cotton-wool bud. The presence of wax may mean that your cat is infected with ear mites, the symptoms of which are brownish lumps and deposits of wax-like substance in the external ear. Other signs are that the cat scratches itself constantly and

bends its ear. The cat should be taken to the vet, who will probably prescribe ear-drops which will get rid of the parasites. If administered properly – the drops are put into the ear and gently massaged in so that the product spreads evenly within the ear – the itching will stop within a few days.

If you find little wounds or crusty scabs in your cat's ear, ask the vet for a disinfecting ointment to prevent the wound becoming infected.

Eyes

Some cats have problems with their tear ducts which produce excessive amounts of

fluid and 'run'. This leads to the formation of crusts or 'sleep' in the corner of the eye. Because the cat cannot reach his eyes easily to clean them and remove the 'sleep', it is up to you to clean the cat's eyes for it. Wipe the rims of its eyes regularly with a soft cloth.

If the eye is actually infected, or if the nictitating membrane (the horizontal moving membrane) is visible, or if the eyes are red, you must go to the vet and ask advice in case it is a serious infection.

Teeth

Kittens get their milk teeth at the age of two to three months and three months later they grow their permanent teeth – 30 of them – which in most cats remain healthy until quite a late age. Caries (tooth decay) is quite unusual in cats. However, older cats become prone to plaque with leads to the build-up of tartar and gingivitis or infection of the gums which is very painful. You will know if your cat is suffering from tartar on its teeth because it will develop bad breath, salivate excessively (perhaps even with blood) and – in the very worst cases – it will refuse to eat. Tartar is yellow to grey in appearance and sticks to the surface of the teeth. As also-happens with humans, the build-up of tartar leads to pressure on the teeth while the bacteria which accumulate in the tartar leads to inflammation of the gums (gingivitis) and the mouth cavity(stomatitis). As a result the gums begin to recede; they become bright red and bleed easily. If these infections are not treated immediately and the tartar removed, the teeth will start to loosen and eventually fall out.

Before following the tips for the treatment of tartar, first take the cat to the vet and ask for its mouth to be checked because gingivitis and stomatitis can also be caused by other illnesses. When you go to have your cat vaccinated, it is worth asking the vet to inspect the cat's teeth and gums in any case because the surgery will have the right instruments to remove the tartar.

Because not all cats are willing to have their teeth inspected, the vet will give a light anaesthetic before removing the tartar with a special instruments. Your cat may allow you to remove the tartar yourself: scratch the loose tartar away with your nail and then clean your cat's teeth regularly.

Ask your vet how best to look after your cat's teeth. Give your cat 'hard' food so that it has something to bite on as this will help prevent the build-up of plaque and tartar. Solid pieces of meat and dry food like cat biscuits will keep your cat's teeth healthy because they have to chew hard and this chewing makes the jaws stronger.

In addition, it is important to clean your cat's teeth and gums regularly. The only problem is that cats do not like having their teeth cleaned, especially if they have not been not used to it since they were little kittens.

There are also antiseptic mouth rinses and toothpastes which can be applied to the teeth and gums to protect against gum disease.

General hygiene

To prevent diseases and parasites, the litter tray, sleeping area and scratching pole should be cleaned and disinfected regularly. Wash – or rather boil – the blanket and cushion on which your cat usually sleeps, change the contents of the litter tray completely twice a day and rinse the litter tray in hot water with a cleaning agent to kill all the bacteria.

The scratching pole can be washed in the shower but all the cat's hair should be removed beforehand. You must vacuum-clean all the corners, armchairs and sofas on which the cat sits.

During the first few weeks, the mother cat will look after the cleanliness of its kittens by licking their hair clean every day

The most important cat diseases and their treatment:

When the cat is ill

*Cats love
to roll and
stretch on
the ground;
it is a sign
of health
and
happiness*

Luckily, not every change in a cat's bodily functions means that it is ill. For instance, diarrhoea may simply be caused by food which the cat did not digest, such as raw meat or milk. All that is needed is to change the cat's diet until the diarrhoea stops. The same is true of constipation. This may be caused, for instance, by hairballs, formed by the hair swallowed by the cat while cleaning itself, which hardens in the stomach and bowels. A little olive oil or oil from a tin of sardines, or even better a special malt paste will be helpful in the case of constipation.

Cats may also vomit quite often. Food they are not used to, cold food, eating too quickly or eating pieces of meat which are too large can also make the cat sick.

A healthy cat has shiny hair, clear eyes and solid muscles. Its normal body temperature is somewhere between 38 and 39° C (100 to 102° F) and, as with all small mammals, a cat's heart beats relatively fast, between 120 and 140 beats per minute.

Cats are quite tough animals. It is only when they are seriously ill that they show it. If you know your cat well, you will immediately notice when it is not well. The following symptoms indicate that everything is not well with your cat: dull, runny eyes, discharge from the mouth or nose, lustreless, tangled or dry hair, spots and lumps on the skin and in the hair, weakness and apathy but also restlessness or

unusual aggression and continuous meowing. If, in addition, the cat also has a temperature, breathing difficulties, coughing or discernible pain, you must not hesitate to take it to the vet.

Without wanting to frighten you and turn you into a hypochondriac so far as your cat is concerned, the more common and widespread diseases of cats will now be described. There are also cat books which concentrate entirely on diseases specific to cats. When reading such books, the tendency is to imagine that your cat has the symptoms of many different diseases so that you worry all the time. But relax: cats are very resistant, robust animals. If they are well fed

*But if the
cat is ill you
must take it
to the vet for
diagnosis
and
treatment*

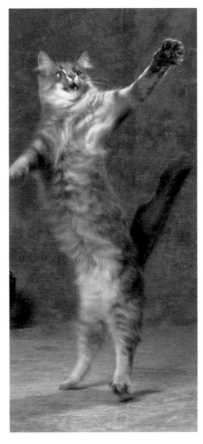

other animals with which the cat does not get on.

Another sensible preventive measure is to visit the vet regularly. They have the knowledge and experience to discover insidious diseases and deficiencies. Annual visits will be sufficient for healthy cats. At the same

and well cared for, they are rarely ill and live to a ripe old age. According to superstition, cats have nine lives, which is supposed to mean that you do not need to worry about them because nature always sorts things out. This is often exactly what happens, but it can be dangerous treatment for a sick cat. So keep an eye on your cat in case!

There is no doubt that prevention is better than a cure.

As well as strict basic hygiene, careful grooming and a healthy diet, the psychological condition of your cat is also important. Cats under stress are more prone to illness than cats which live in peaceful surroundings. Stress factors include noise, scolding and the presence of

time the vet will also vaccinate your cat against viral infectious diseases. This is very important because, unlike bacteria which can be treated with antibiotics, there is no effective treatment against viral infections. Once the virus has entered the

body, the disease and infrequently the death of the animal are pre-programmed and inevitable. In the case of rabies, the health and life of people are also threatened. Besides rabies (except in Britain and Australasia), cats should also be vaccinated against feline infectious enteritis, respiratory viral infection (cat flu) and feline leukaemia virus.

Only a very healthy cat will play and leap about like this

Viral diseases

Rabies:

Rabies does not occur in Britain or Australasia, but it is endemic in most parts of the world and in some it can become epidemic. Also known as hydrophobia and lyssa, it is a very dangerous, infectious viral disease which has been rampant among wild and domestic animals for a very long time. The animals most at risk from rabies are dogs, foxes, wolves and cats. But others such as cows, bulls, horses, sheep, goats, red deer, wild boars and bats can also become infected. Rabies is usually transmitted through a bite, or more rarely through contact with saliva.

The waiting-room at the vet's surgery is not just a place where people wait with their pets – they will also exchange stories and experiences

There are two kinds of symptoms:
– 'Mad' rabies whose symptoms are extreme behavioural changes, irritability, snapping at other animals and restlessness. In addition, there is an increased flow of saliva and difficulties in swallowing. The disease can drag on for weeks. In the final stages, the animal becomes paralysed and finally dies.
– 'Dumb' rabies, where the animal is quiet and afraid of light. It crawls away and becomes apathetic. Wild animals appear trusting but for this reason 'tame' foxes and the like should be avoided. Paralysis appears at an early stage and the

animal usually dies after three to five days.

Anyone who suspects that their cat has been bitten by a rabid animal must immediately go to the doctor. He is legally obliged to inform the veterinary authorities because rabies is a dangerous, notifiable disease. It will then be established on the basis of the animal's vaccination certificate whether it is still protected by the vaccine. The last vaccination must have been given between four weeks and one year before the incident. If this is not the case, the animal will be put into quarantine. If the animal turns out to be rabid, the authorities will require that he is put down.

Because there is no cure after the symptoms have appeared, anyone who suspects that they may have been in contact with a rabid animal must contact a doctor as soon as possible.

Feline infectious enteritis (FIE)

Also known as feline parvovirus, panleukopenia, infectious distemper, cat plague, cat typhoid, enteritis infectiosa or agranulocytosis, this is a viral infection. The variety of names reflects its complexity which is one of the commonest and most dangerous cat diseases. This tenacious virus can survive for

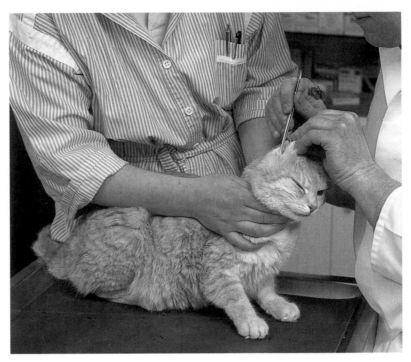

The vet also examines the cat's ears for ticks because they can be very irritating for the cat

months. The virus is transmitted from cat to cat but also through contact with objects such as blankets, cushions, covers, shoes and clothes which have come into contact with the infected cat. The symptoms will appear two to seven days after the infection took place. These symptoms include a high fever with a temperature of up to 40° C (104° F), loss of appetite, diarrhoea, ruffled hair and vomiting.

The cat will only survive if the symptoms are recognised immediately and treated without delay. The vet will do a blood test to confirm the diagnosis, because the pathogen visibly destroys the white blood cells. The destruction of the white blood cells weakens the immune system so that the animal's body may not be able to resist further infections such as pneumonia, pleurisy and peritonitis.

It is very important to treat the symptoms immediately. Fasting is absolutely necessary for 48 hours. If the cat responds, it may then be given broth, fluid, soup or glucose dissolved in water. In order to boost the immune system, the cat is also given antibiotics, vitamins (preferably the B-group vitamins) and injected with the serum from the blood of cats which have had the illness and survived it In spite of all the

treatments, the mortality rate of cats which catch FIE is still the highest of all cat diseases, between 80% and 90%.

If the cat survives FIE, it will be immune to the disease for the rest of its life. But after the cat's recovery all the rooms, the cat's bed and all the objects with which the cat has been in contact must be disinfected. Covers, blankets and cushions are best burnt. But in spite of thorough disinfection, the virus may still lurk somewhere, so the possibility of infection remains. This means that at least three months should elapse before another cat is introduced into the house.

Feline viral rhinotracheitis (FVR)

Also known as cat flu, feline viral rhinotracheitis is the second most common cat disease. It is usually transmitted by a variety of pathogens. The

name 'cat flu' may sound rather harmless but the disease is very serious and completely unrelated to human influenza. The first symptoms are sneezing, runny nose and watering eyes. If left untreated, the disease can go on for weeks and even months and often ends with the death of the animal. Even if the cat does not die, it will be left with life-long nose and paranasal sinus problems. The disease can last between two and four weeks and is accompanied by fever, a suppurating discharge from the eyes and nose, and inflammation of the mouth and throat. Besides these symptoms, the cat may also suffer from pneumonia and womb infections as well as nervous disorders.

Feline calcivirus (FCR) is another very serious respiratory disease.

As with FIE, treatment of both involves boosting the

immune system is boosted by antibiotics and vitamins. Other treatment involves cleaning the eyes and nose carefully cleaned with warm salted water, after which soothing ointments are applied.

In spite of careful treatment many cases of cat flu

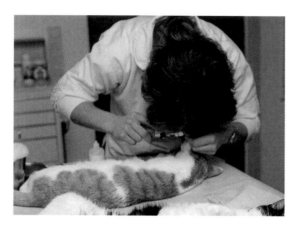

become chronic, which means that the paranasal sinuses have been permanently damaged. In that case the sinuses must be opened up from the outside in order to clean them daily. However, the survival rates are higher than for FIE, so long as the cat is immediately taken to the vet to receive the right treatment.

Feline leukaemia virus (FeLV)

Also known as cat leukaemia, this is a weakening of the immune system caused by the feline leukaemia virus (FLV). The virus only affects cats and cannot transmitted

to humans. Many of the affected cats – about 80% – die within three years. The disease is transmitted from cat to cat through saliva, urine and excrement. The clinical picture of cat leukaemia is diverse. The symptoms can vary from apathy, extreme diarrhoea and severe loss of weight to anaemia, pneumonia, jaundice and cancerous growths. These symptoms are often accompanied by chronic maxillary sinusitis and kidney infections.

The disease is further complicated by its so-called time-bomb effects. This means that the cat may have been infected for years without showing any symptoms. During this time the virus may have been transmitted to other cats without any one realising it.

In recent years, a vaccine has been developed against

cat leukaemia which should be administered in two stages at the age of 12 weeks, and 16 weeks, followed by annual boosters.

Feline infectious peritonitis (FIP)

Feline infectious peritonitis (FIP) is also known as abdominal dropsy; it is usually fatal. It is transmitted by contact with an infected cat but also through contact with an infected cat's litter tray, brushes and feeding-bowls. The early symptoms are chronic fever, loss of appetite, loss of weight, followed by the accumulation of fluid in the abdomen, thoracic cavity and pericardium. Almost every organ will be affected by the disease, the kidneys, spleen and liver being the most commonly affected. The eyes and nervous system can also be damaged by it.

Feline immunodeficiency virus (FIV)

Although not common, feline immunodeficiency virus (FIV) is very serious because it is incurable and there is no vaccination against it. This virus is related to the AIDS-virus (HIV) but it cannot be transmitted from cats to humans. The disease is usually transmitted through a bite; infection through mating has not yet been proved.

Cats who are at risk are ones which live with other animals or which live outside a lot where cats often fight and bite. In some cases many years can go by after the cat has been infected with the virus before the disease break out. It attacks the lymph glands and weakens the immune system. This is followed by an infection of the gums and mucus membrane of the mouth, infection of the urinary tract, the skin and the

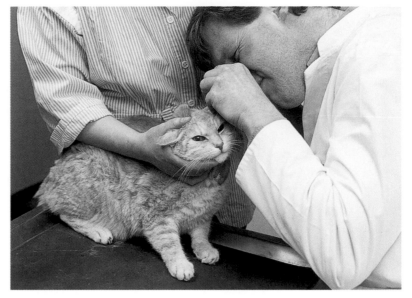

Ordinary wax deposits in the cat's outer ear are easily removed with a soft, flexible cotton bud. But if you notice any parasites, you should ask the vet's advice

respiratory tract. The cat also frequently suffers from diarrhoea and nervous disorders, the lymph nodes become affected and the kidneys stop functioning. As with HIV, there is no successful cure for FIV. Only the symptoms can be treated.

Vaccination programme

The importance of vaccination is self-evident and the table below gives a recommended vaccination programme for cats. The vet will advise on the best vaccines for your cat and administer them.

Some of the vaccines available to combat the various viral infections are combined which makes the vaccination process simpler. FVRCP is a combination of FIE, FVR and FCV vaccines.

The protection given by the vaccination can be influenced by several factors – the health of the cat, de-worming and incorrect timing of the vaccination. It is vital that your cat has the second (booster) injection after the initial vaccination and that it is given the annual booster vacccinations. On the other hand, too many vaccinations given at the same time can weaken the cat. The vet's advice should therefore be followed.

Before undertaking a journey, check the date of the cat's vaccinations and all the conditions of entry for the

Basic immuisation:

8 weeks:	FVRCP (against FIE, FVR and FCV)
12 weeks:	FVRCP booster FeLV (againt feline leukemia)
16 weeks:	FeLV booster; FVRCP booster (if advised) FIP (if advised)
19 weeks:	FIP booster

Booster vaccinations:

annual:	FVRCP and FIP

117

country concerned. Many require immunisation against rabies within a particular time limit, and quarantine regulations may apply.

Parasites

Toxoplasmosis

The parasite toxoplasma gondii attacks the cat's mucous membrane and causes small blisters on the inner organs. The parasite also produces millions of so-called oocystes in the cat's excre-

A special collar, known as an Elizabethan collar, prevents the cat scratching and licking its wounds

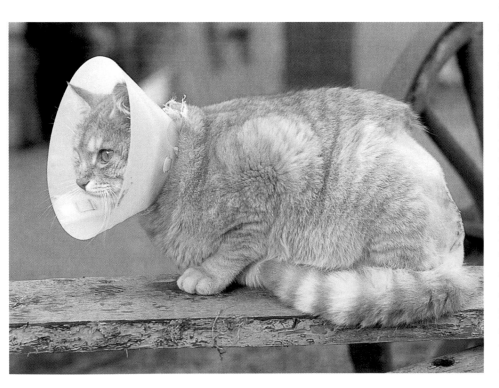

ment which are invisible to the human eye. Cats become infected with toxoplasmosis through intermediate hosts such as mice but also raw meat. Even when cats are not seriously ill with toxoplasmosis – a little diarrhoea is the only visible symptom – the litter tray of infected cats should be disinfected and the excrement checked daily. As a preventive measure, the cat should not eat any raw meat. Humans may also become infected with the parasite but usually as result of eating raw pork and lamb meat, and only rarely through contact with cat's excrement when dealing with the litter tray. Toxoplasmosis does not cause serious health problems in most people but it can have

serious consequences for an unborn baby, so pregnant women should not deal with the cat's litter tray.

Worms:

Roundworms, hookworms and tapeworms are transmitted through their eggs and are often the cause of serious metabolic disorders. Only roundworms and tapeworms can be seen with the naked eye, either in the cat's excrement or when it is sick. Regular de-worming of the cat is effective against these parasites, but it is not a preventive measure because it only kills the worms already present in the cat's intestines.

Fleas:

The eggs laid by the fleas in the cat's hair fall off and are scattered wherever the cat goes. This means that flea eggs and larvae can be found anywhere in the home. Flea bites causes skin infections and itching. Flea-collars, flea powder, insecticide and the thorough cleaning of all the places where the cat usually sits are the best ways of combating a flea epidemic. It is particularly important to use a disinfectant where cleaning with water and detergent is not possible. If necessary, a spray to use on carpets and in the gaps can be obtained. This cleaning and disinfecting of the cat's surroundings is absolutely necessary because the flea collar merely helps the cat get rid of the fleas; the eggs and larvae are not destroyed.

Other diseases

Dermatomycosis:
Microsporum and trichophyton fungi scatter their spores everywhere in the home and after a month or two will lead to loss of hair, scales and crusts on the cat's skin. All you can do is to clean the places where the cat sits and sleeps and the toys it plays with. To treat the illness itself, the cat must be taken to the vet who will make a diagnosis and treat it accordingly. The danger of fungal infection should not be underestimated because it can also be transmitted to humans.

Abscess (boil or furuncle)
Abscesses occur when a poisonous or foreign substance has entered the body. The body fights against this invasion, more blood flows towards the affected tissues, and the white blood cells try to expel the poison through the skin. This is why an abscess should never be squeezed because that drives the poison or pus back into

the blood stream. An abscess causes the affected area to swell; it becomes hot, the skin turns red and it is very painful.

To treat an abscess place a clean cloth dipped in warm salted water on the affected area. Continue for 10 to15 minutes, then dry the area Repeat the operation after a few hours. If the paw or leg of the cat is affected, dip the entire limb in the warm, salted water.

Take the animal to the vet when the abscess is 'ripe'. The vet will then decide whether to lance the abscess or to wait until it bursts of its own accord, the infected area being bathed at home until it does so. In severe cases, penicillin may be used to combat the infection.

If the abscess bursts, continue with the compresses but replace the salt with hydrogen peroxide for the first 2 or 3 dressings. This clears the pus and neutralises the smell. It will also stop the cat from licking the wound. After a while, the wound should be left uncovered and moist so that the pus can come out.

Eye infections
If your cat's eye is infected, do not use eye ointment immediately; it may cause more trouble than it solves. First you should try washing the eye very carefully, using a

solution of 600 ml (1 pint) water with one teaspoon of salt. If the infection is caused by the presence of small foreign body in the eye, this will be very helpful.

But most eye infections are not independent problems; frequently they are symptoms of other illnesses. If

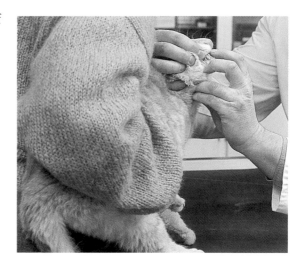

there is no improvement after 1 or 2 days of the salt water bathing, you should go to the vet to establish and treat the cause. The same is true of conjunctivitis which may also be the symptom of another illness.

*A cat should
have a
general
examination
by a vet
once a year*

Bladder infection or cystitis
If your cat produces increasingly small amounts of urine and afterwards appears to strain and emit sounds of pain, it may be suffering from a bladder infection. The urine could have a foul smell and may be blood-stained. If this

is the case, you should immediately consult the vet since the cat may be suffering from feline urological syndrome. A urine test will establish whether your cat is suffering from this or some other bladder infection.

The usual treatment is a course of antibiotics and

Older cats often suffer from bad teeth as a result of tartar and plaque, the main cause of gum disease. In the most serious cases, some teeth may have to be removed while the rest of the teeth are thoroughly cleaned

application of a bladder antiseptic which will cure the animal in about 2 weeks.

If the cat is suffering from feline urological syndrome, the vet will prescribe a diet to discourage the formation of urinary stones and to dissolve them. Stones in the bladder or urethra occur mainly in tom cats because even tiny particles of grit can block the penis. If your tom cat appears bloated and tries to urinate without success, pick it up carefully and take it immediately to the vet. A blockage of the urethra may be life-threatening and requires prompt intervention.

Mammary gland tumour:
These tumours usually appear in the region of the chest and belly near the nipples in non-spayed female cats which have never had a litter. Such tumours should never be ignored and should be examined by a vet within 1 or 2 days of their appearance because they can grow very quickly. Prompt surgical intervention will usually solve the problem.

Diabetes mellitus:
One of the earliest symptoms of diabetes are a greater thirst and increased appetite, to the point of ravenous hunger. But in spite of eating large amounts of food the cat becomes increasingly thin,

which is the classic symptom of diabetes. This is the result of an insulin deficiency, caused by the destruction of the insulin-forming cells in the pancreas.

Diabetes can be diagnosed by a blood or urine test. If the tests prove positive, the cat must given daily insulin injections under the skin. The operation can be simplified by using special semi-automatic insulin injections which will enable even those with no experience of injecting to give the cat its necessary insulin injections.

Diet also plays an important part in the management of diabetes. The diet of a diabetic cat must be such that it prevents excessive fluctuations in blood sugar levels. For this purpose, specially developed fibre-rich food with complex carbohydrates and very little fat can be obtained from the vet.

There are also other types of diabetes besides insulin-dependent diabetes. In cats, there is the so-called stress-related or temporary diabetes. This type of diabetes occurs when stress hormones are produced as a result of a viral infection. These stress hormones counteracts the insulin, which is prevented from breaking down the sugar. When the cat is well again, the stress hormones disappear and the insulin begins to work again. A blood test to establish the level of fructasamine in the blood will help identify this type of diabetes.

There is another type of diabetes which occurs in older, overweight cats. This type of diabetes is managed simply by following a special diet without the need for daily insulin injections.

What to do if your cat should have a serious accident

If your cat should be seriously injured, urgent measures will be necessary to save its life. Most injuries are the result of traffic accidents or falling from an open window. Serious accidents can result in open wounds, broken bones, other injuries and trauma.

Should you find your own cat (or any other one) seriously injured, you must be very careful in handling it, because a cat which is in pain will refuse to be touched and it will fight back if you try to do so.

If an object has pierced or entered the cat's body, do not try to remove it – that must be left to the vet. If you think the cat may have broken a bone, do not touch or move the part of the cat's body where the fracture is suspected, and certainly do not attempt to apply a splint

yourself. Just cover the cat with a blanket to keep it as warm as possible and to counteract the effects of the trauma on its circulation. Then take the animal immediately to the vet.

In the case of an open wound, you should try and stop the bleeding by gently pressing a clean cloth or gauze to the injured area. Even if the wound is small, it is important to take the cat to the vet because there could be internal injuries and the wound might have become infected. This could be very dangerous because a serious infecton can cause death because of the accompanying fever.

An injured cat must be transported very carefully so as not to aggravate any fractures or other injuries. Slip a towel under the cat's body before you lift it – this will stabilise the cat's position. Then very gently lift the cat with the towel on which it is lying with both arms while supporting its back. Place the cat carefully in a container and take it to the vet as quickly as possible.

The vet will explain how to look after your cat after an operation and how to tend to its injuries – always follow the vet's instructions to ensure the successful outcome of the treatment. These will include changing its

dressings and giving its his medication if you do not wish to depend on the vet for the cat's aftercare.

The cost of veterinary and other treatment for your cat in the event of accidents or serious illness can be very high. For this reason, when you acquire your cat it is

A plaster cast is often needed while a broken bone mends

worth giving serious consideration to taking out a health insurance policy for it. The premiums may seem high, but it could save money in the end. Your vet will be able to give you information.

Some injuries need protecting from infection by an overall dressing, which also helps it heal quicker

Special tips for

special situations

When your cat is expecting kittens

Cats reach sexual maturity at between six to twelve months in the case of females and eight months in the case of males. However, it is not advisable for a cat to have a litter before the age of one year because it would put too much strain on its body.

After a gestation period of 2 months, a cat will give

and also give them all the necessary, loving maternal care. The kittens will also learn many things from their mother which are important for their survival. By imitating their mother the kittens will learn all the sequences of movements and skills they need to be independent. It is true that their climbing skills are determined by their physique, but it is by observing the skills of their mother

From a medical point of view, it is relatively easy to look after young kittens. The mother will bring its young into the world on its own without direct assistance. It usually chooses a quiet, hidden corner in a familiar place.

Nonetheless, cat owners who want to breed from their cat will find it quite a time-consuming exercise. On the one hand, they must look after the mother-to-be and provide all the necessary care. Then later the kittens will need plenty of attention. In other words, from the time the cat comes into season to the birth of the kittens – a period of about five months – both mother and kittens will require a lot of time and attention.

Obviously, the female cat must be mated while on heat in order to become pregnant. Whether the mating has been successful will be apparent by about the 3rd week of pregnancy. The mother-to-be should be given additional proteins, vitamins and minerals and the number of meals

This Siamese cat has three delightful kittens, about 10 weeks old

birth to about four kittens which will each weigh about 100 g (4 oz). If the mother is too young, the kittens will be born earlier and smaller, after about 55 days and weighing only 70 g (3 oz).

The kittens must stay with mother until the age of 12 weeks. She will suckle them

that the young kitten learns to hunt, climb and balance.

Small kittens which are allowed to take their first steps in life and to join their mother on its hunting expeditions will be much more skilful in their movements than cats who are removed too early from their mother.

*Right:
Theoretically, a
healthy female cat
can produce 200
sweet little kittens like
these in its lifetime*

The birth of a kitten usually takes place without complications

should be increased from three to four a day.

By about the 7th week, the pregnant cat will begin to look for a place where she can 'nest' and give birth. Shut the doors of all the rooms and places where you do not want the young to be born and keep them closed.

Help the cat by providing satisfactory alternatives. A warm, snug, not too bright room with a comfortable basket, sofa or cupboard are ideal places for the cat to give birth and for the kittens to live in during the first three months. The place must not be draughty and it should be softly upholstered and nest-like, because cats like to withdraw to give birth.

Humans should be very careful and gentle with newborn kittens so that the little creatures learn to trust them

Two or three days before the birth the cat's nipples will become even more enlarged

and the milk begins to come in. Cats which are very close to their owners constantly seek their company during pregnancy and especially during labour. They want to be reassured and stroked.

Contractions of increasing rapidity are followed by the breaking of the waters and the birth of the kittens. Usually the cat does not not need any help from its owner; let it give birth in peace. You should only notify the vet and ask for advice if the kittens still have not been born two or three hours after the onset of labour and contractions. Fortunately, complications are rare when cats give birth.

The kittens are born in a mucous membrane which is removed by the mother by licking, a process which also cleans the kittens. If the mother forgets to clean one, you can help. Cut the umbilical cord 1 cm (⅜ in) above the navel, remove the mucous membrane and briefly stroke the kitten before handing it back to its mother.

Remain nearby during the birth, even if it is lengthy; it can vary between half an hour and six hours.

It is easy to determine the sex of the kittens in the first two days of their life because they have no hair yet. In female cats, the anus and vagina are close together, while in male cats, the anus is closer to the base of the tail and the anus and sexual organs are further apart. In male cats both openings below the base of the tail look like two round dots while in female cats the appearance is of a dot (anus) with a line underneath (vagina).

If the mother has been eating well and continues to do so, she will have plenty of milk to feed all the young for

Your cat should feel comfortable and happy in your holiday flat or villa, although it may not enjoy the journey much. But they would normally be even happier staying in their usual surroundings

the first two weeks. From the 3rd week onwards the kittens will already be eating some solid food, although they will still be relying on their mother's milk for the major part of their diet. A wide range of ready-made cat food is available, including some which has been specially developed to satisfy the needs of very young kittens – not too coarse or hard and enriched with the right nutrients. These are widely available.

To make sure that the kittens soon get used to people, they should be gently stroked on a regular basis. Naturally, any contact with the kittens (including the determination of sex) should only take place if the mother's behaviour indicates acceptance.

Vaccination should normally be carried out eight and twelve weeks after the birth. The young kittens should not be taken away from their mother before they are 12 weeks old.

Travelling with a cat

All cat owners worry about what to do when they go away. Should the beloved pet be entrusted to a neighbour or friend, or should it be put in a cattery, or can it come on holiday with them?

It has already been mentioned that this aspect of owning a cat should be considered and resolved before acquiring one.

So far as travelling overseas is concerned, there are complicated procedures to be complied with. It is vital to assess these before you decide whether or not to take your pet with you abroad.

If travelling from the UK, you must find out the requirements of the destination country or countries. Many will require a valid certificate of inoculation against rabies and some require a comprehensive health certificate.

But the even more serious thing to consider is the

return journey. Unless it is eligible and complies with the PETS scheme (described below), any pet entering Britain has to spend six months in quarantine. It is almost certain that both you and your cat would suffer greatly from this lengthy enforced separation, and the cost of keeping the cat in quarantine premises is substantial.

Recently the UK has introduced the Pet Travel Scheme (PETS). This enables cats (and dogs) to visit qualifying countries – which include most of the countries in

Europe – and return to the UK without having to spend six months in quarantine, provided other conditions are complied with. The cat must be fitted with a microchip to enable it to be identified; it must be vaccinated against rabies; it must have a blood test to test that the rabies vaccination gives a satisfactory

Some cats do genuinely enjoy their holidays when the weather and the garden are just right

**Special
tips for
special
situations**

*Feral cats in
many
countries
welcome
the company
of passing
tourists who
often give
them the
left-overs of
their picnic*

level of protection against rabies.

Between 24 and 48 hours of entering the UK again, the cat must be treated against ticks and tapeworm, and issued with an official certificate showing that this treatment has been carried out. The owner must sign a declaration of residency relating to the cat.

Finally, only nominated sea, rail or air PETS routes may be used to bring the pet back into the UK.

So, although the new system avoids the need for quarantine in some circumstances, it is complicated, and it is essential that all the conditions be meticulously complied with.

Once you are prepared for any the formalities, you must decide whether a long journey would be too much for your cat, whether by car, train or plane. Would the excitement of travelling by plane in a cat carrier prove too much ? Some airlines allow a pet in a carrier to

travel as hand luggage. The cat will also be much happier to know that you are nearby. Otherwise the cat will have to travel in the hold, which would be terrible for the cat. The darkness and noise are not a suitable environment for a cat and will put it under enormous stress, as will travelling along the baggage

conveyor, on which the carrier will be tumbled in all directions, frequently in the dark.

The next problem is where your cat will stay when arrive at your destination – a hotel room is not really suitable for a cat which will be very bored by being confined to one room. It would also be difficult and expensive to find a hotel that will allow you to bring in the cat's litter tray and scratching pole.

A caravan holiday would be much better proposition for a cat, which would probably find it very enjoyable and exciting. You too would find it much more relaxing: you are surrounded by your own

*They are also quite partial
to a little cuddling*

things and you can arrange the caravan in such a way that the cat recognises its environment. With a long lead, your cat will be able to explore the surroundings and satisfy its curiosity. It should also be mentioned that most camping-sites allow pets and that on many sites pets are allowed to wander freely. It is therefore not unusual for pets to pay their neighbours a visit!

The conclusion is that going on holiday with your cat is really only practical if you travel by car to a rented a flat or villa, or with a caravan.

Once all conditions for a holiday with your cat have been met, you can start packing your cat's luggage. It is not always possible to buy its favourite food at your destination, so supplies should be brought with you. You should also bring its blanket, feeding and drinking bowls, flea collar and so on, as well as s small first aid kit.

It is also sensible to find out the address of the nearest vet as soon as you arrive.

Although your cat may like to wander about at home you cannot allow it this kind of

Caravan sites can be excellent places for taking your cat on holiday with you. They can roam around under your supervision or just lie lazily in the sun

freedom on the caravan site or in your holiday home. The new surroundings may upset and confuse your cat and it might get lost. So it should only be allowed to explore outside on a lead – a cat needs at least two weeks to get used to its new surroundings and find its way back to its new home.

*Cats hate
moving to a
new house
or flat. All
the familiar
furniture
disappears
into a van,
and then
they have to
adjust to
their new
surroundings*

Moving – an unnerving experience for the cat

Moving to a new house or flat with a cat is not easy. It is not practical to lock up your cat in a room for a whole day to stop it being in the way of the removal men. The cat does not enjoy the unusual hectic atmosphere either; the presence of the removal men who are strangers and the

moving of furniture are very disturbing for a cat.

Then, in the new home the cat finds itself in completely new surroundings which make it feel uneasy.

If the removal also involves changes in the cat's living conditions, the problem is even greater because it may need to be taught new habits and patterns of behaviour. For instance, if your cat has been accustomed to roaming around and this is not possible in your new home, it will be very difficult to persuade it never to go out! If it is used to chasing mice and exploring the surrounding countryside it will not understand why this is

*A little snooze is always
a welcome relief from
the stressful situation of
moving to a new home*

no longer possible in its new urban surroundings. It will howl for hours and scratch at the door to get out. Apart from the damage, this is very bad for the cat's nerves. You must be patient and wait till your cat accepts his new situation – which should be after a few weeks.

On the other hand, it is much easier to train a cat which is not used to going outside to wander out.

The trauma of moving can be minimised with the help of a few tips. Organise the removal to cause the least distress and get the cat used to the new home and the unknown surroundings. Do not let your cat go out on the day of the removal, put it a closed room - with everything he needs - so that he cannot hide in the boxes or be in the way of the removal men. When all the furniture has been loaded onto the van, release your cat from his 'prison'.

When you arrive in your new home, do not let the cat wander about the house or flat. Choose one room which has been arranged to a certain degree and leave the cat there until the last of the boxes has been brought into the house. Then try and recreate the surroundings the cat was used to and show it more affection. This will show that at least one thing

has not have changed: even though everything else is new, you are still there! If your cat is not of a timid disposition, it will soon be exploring its new surroundings and settling down in its new home. A less confident cats will immediately look for a little corner where it can hide and feel safe, since it finds the new home strange and unfriendly. But after a

to explore its new surroundings, wait at least two weeks before allowing it to go out. Any earlier than this, it may get lost or try to run away to its old home, because it has not yet accepted its new one.

A strong bond with its owner will reduce the distress a cat suffers after moving to new home. But the presence of a 'sibling', another cat, is often the best distraction.

couple of weeks most cats will have settled down happily and will have forgotten all about the removal.

So that your cat does not get lost when it goes outside

After moving into its new home, the cat observes its surroundings. From its raised position it can survey the situation and locate the best places in its new home while feeling secure.

Avoiding accidents and preventing wandering cats running away

Cats which wander about a lot are constantly surrounded by many life-threatening dangers and cat owners must be prepared for the fact that one day their beloved pet may not return. Speeding cars, cat-hating neighbours, other animals, professional thieves and structural dangers may all be fatal to cats.

Although they cannot necessarily guarantee a long life, there are several steps you can take to help keep your cat healthy. Remember the times your cat normally goes out.

When they are outside cats are much more cautious than they are in the home. If they see a person or animal they do not recognise, they will retreat and study the situation safely from behind some bushes

Guided by its internal body clock, it will normally always come and go at the same time.

It will probably take your cat about two weeks to get used to its new home

Never make your cat wait to be let out or let in. Ideally, you should have a cat-flap so that your cat can come and go without your help. This will be much easier for you and your cat which will not only enjoy greater freedom, it will also appreciate the welcome facility of being able to run back into the house if threatened by danger. However, a cat-flap means that there may be unwelcome visitors, unless you have the kind activated by a magnet hanging on your cat's collar.

A cat-flap also solves the problem for owners who are out at work all day, since the cat cannot be locked out all day even if it loves being out and about. In bad weather, for instance, it will much prefer sitting in a warm place indoors to chasing mice.

Another solution may be to get your cat used to going out at night. In this way, you

*Most cats love wandering about
in the open, but the outside world
is full of unexpected dangers*

can let it out late at night and
let it in again in the morning
before going to work. There is
the added advantage that
there is much less traffic at
night and the cat will find it
easier to hide if it feels threatened by danger. On the other
hand, you will see very little
of your cat.

In general, whether you
allow your cat to go out or
not depends entirely on you
and your living conditions.
You alone can weigh up the
advantages and the risks of
letting your cat roam outside
on its own. If you do decide

to let your cat go out, make
sure there is a tag on its collar
with your name, address and
telephone number on it so
that anyone finding it lost
can return it.

*Out of doors in the warm sun,
a cat really knows how to relax*

Rights and disputes over keeping cats

If you live in rented accommodation, it is advisable and necessary check that you are allowed to have a pet so as to avoid misunderstandings and legal disputes between the landlord and tenant. Some tenancy agreements forbid pets altogether, and others specify that the written permission of the landlord must be obtained. Even owner-occupied properties may be subject to covenants restricting the right to keep pets.

Apart from the conditions of such agreements and covenants, no-one – not even neighbours who dislike pets – is entitled to object to a reasonable number of pets being kept, so long as they do not cause a serious nuisance which might breach an individual's rights. Remember that any differences are best resolved by negotiation. Legal proceedings should be avoided wherever possible,

Before getting a cat, you must check that pets aer allowed where you live. This cat rules over its territory with authority, supremely confident of its right to be there

being costly, uncertain, emotionally draining and seldom satisfactory even when concluded.

Watch out where your cat likes to sleep if it goes out. Some cats like to sleep on cars, but this can antagonise the owner who fears that the paint may be damaged by the cat scratching the paint. In fact such damage is never caused by cats, because the smooth surface of a car is completely unsuitable for sharpening claws, and apart from that reason they never use their claws against inanimate objects. But car owners may not know this, and they are likely to be unwilling to believe it even if they are

told. In the worst situation they may demand compensation from you for damage done they claim – wrongly – has been caused by your cat; or they may take direct action against the cat. So the best solution is to discourage your car from sitting on cars.

Cats are widely believed to be responsible for the death of large numbers of garden birds. But it is an established fact that cats seldom succeed in catching healthy birds; even in the case of farm cats in the country, over 90% of birds chased will escape, and the success rate of a pampered town cat is likely to be subtantially less.

In general, it can be said

that cats only catch brids which have already been injured. So it is unreasonable to accuse cats of causing the reduction of the bird population in gardens, parks and the countryside.

Some bird lovers also believe that song birds stay away from gardens where there are cats because they are afraid of them. This theory too has never been proved. Although it is true that birds are easily frightened, they are also very good at assessing danger. They do not usually fly away when they see a cat near them; they only do so if they see that the cat is about to attack, and they normally return a little later.

135

Catalogue of

pedigree cats

The characteristics describing the 50 or so different, recognized breeds are defined internationally as standards. These standards are defined by the British *Governing Council of the Cat fancy (GCCF)* and the French *Fédération Internationale Féline (F.I.Fe)* whose regulations are also followed by the *1. Deutscher Edelkatzenzüchterverband e. V.* and

Will I be the Siamese Champion?

This is what will attract the jury's attention and determine a cat's victory.

The highest prizes that a pedigree cat can win are the international title *Certificat d'Aptitude au Championnat d'Europe (CACE)* and the prize awarded by the German Katzen-Union *Certificat d'Aptitude au Grand Championnat d'Europe (CAGCEE)*. All the titles which cats win in exhibitions – from simply 'good' to the *Certificat d'Aptitude au Championnat* (CAC) to the *Certificat d'Aptitude au Grand Championnat International de Beauté* (CAGCIB) are awarded above all for excelling in the qualities of their breed. These exhibitions therefore attract many breeders who look for other pedigree animals to breed with their own cats in order to improve the excellence of the breed. This is why these exhibitions give breeding value to the cats which take part, but they are not 'auctions' at which cats are 'sold' to the highest bidder.

Deutsche Rassekatzen-Union. These two German associations are made up of over 50 smaller and partly also independent cat societies. These societies and associations also provide the jury members for competitions and exhibitions in which the best examples of a breed compete. In these events, it is not the 'noble' pedigree of the cat that matters, but the smoothness, pattern and colour of the fur.

Breeders choose prospective parents with correct markings on their fur

Longhaired cats are very popular

These events are geared to the breeding of cats as a hobby not business.

The cat is first examined by a vet, and if it is declared healthy the members of the jury will study the animal with critical eyes. They will not only take into account the pattern and colour of the fur but they will also note a deformed tail or an obvious

This cat is apparently not interested in the competition

indentation in the cat's forehead. The breeding value of a cat is reduced for instance by dental problems or by too small nostrils which would affect the animal's health. Serious skeletal malformation such as a crooked back, weak knees or missing claws are rarely seen at these exhibitions. Such problems would

result in the disqualification of the animal, since they are features with a seriously negative effect on the cat's health.

Another important aspect in the classification of pedigree cats is whether the cats will allow the members of the jury to examine them without resisting. If they do, it means that they are quiet, human-friendly representatives of their breed. Naturally cats on show must also be excellently groomed.

The system of valuation is based on a series of criteria which are each allocated a number of points out of 100. In a white Persian cat, 25% is awarded for the colour, 20% for the fur, head and body and 15% for the eyes. In other breeds, such as the British Shorthair, the tail, ears and condition – in other words the general appearance of the cat – are taken into account with a different value given for each of these features. A cat which achieves more than 88 points is classified as 'excellent' and ideally suited for breeding. The pedigree of a cat also includes entries such as Champion and International Champion : this means that these cats have been awarded a challenge certificate three times and can now be called champions.

Unlike the situation with

dogs, the breeding of cats is unlikely to turn into a money-spinning business – the breeders invest a lot of time and money in the care and maintenance of these noble animals, and the cost of taking part in these exhibitions is high, with the expense of the journey, entry

This cat is definitely posing for the judges

fees, research into the pedigree of the exhibited animal, and so on. The sale of a pedigree cat will hardly reimburse the breeder for these expenses. Cats are less 'useful' than dogs in that they cannot be used as a guardian of a home or to protect a person; the appeal of cats is more aesthetic. But as with dogs, the breeding of pedigree animals

cat societies and associations formed an umbrella organisation, the Governing Council of the Cat Fancy (GCCF). On a European level, the umbrella organisation Fédération Internationale Féline d'Europe (FIFé) was founded in 1949. A few years later, in 1953, the Edelkatzenzüchter-Verband e.V. (Association of Pedigree Cat Breeders) was established in Germany, and in Britain, the Cat Association of Britain (CA) was founded in 1983.

Cat shows date back as far as 1871. Pedigree cats are less overbred than dogs because it is the coat in which breeders are most interested, rather than physical features.

can lead to overbreeding. However the frequently negative results of selective breeding are less apparent in cats – for instance, pedigree cats have fewer of the health problemswhich often afflict dogs, such as hip malformations.

As already mentioned in the section *When cats became domestic animals*, the British are particularly fond of pedigree cats of Eastern origin. such as Longhairs. Initially angora cats were especially popular among the well-off classes in Britain, Italy and France. Angora is a term which refers to all longhaired cats and rabbits because they came from Turkey (Ankara is derived from the Greek name of the city Angora) but it also included all Persian cats.

Exhibitions and standards defining the breed first came into being in the late 19th century. The first exhibition was organised in London by the Englishman Harrison Weir, who also invented the point system after which the breeds became standardised. The growing enthusiasm of the British for cats, the *Cat Fancy*, led to the foundation of the *National Cat Club* in 1877 and to another society for cat fanciers, *The Cat Club*, in 1889. In 1910, forty years after the first cat exhibitions and competitions, the British

The following pages are devoted to a description of some of the best-known and exotic breeds for which standards have been established by the *Cat Fancy*.

Particular terms are used to describe accurately the many patterns, markings and colours of cats.

Bi-colour is a cat with a coat of white and another colour. *Blaze* describes a longitudinal white line on the cat's fur, running from the forehead

down to the nose. *Cameo* refers to pink-coloured Persian cats, bred by mating red and cream coloured cats. while *Chinchilla* is an ash-grey to white cat. The members of the jury and breeders call large, round, clear eyes *open eyes*. A *hybrid* is a bastard or mongrel, in other words not a pure-bred animal, while *tabby* refers to horizontal or diagonal stripes and marbled markings. *Lilac* is the term used to describe Siamese cats which are white with pinkish-grey points. The dark parts in an

Pedigree cats are often distinguished for the harmonious markings of their beautiful coats.

otherwise light-coloured face is known as a *mask*. The term *tortoiseshell* or *tortie* refers to the female cats with cream, black and brownish markings and other colour combinations. *Silver-shaded* is self-explanatory: the cat's fur has a silvery hue which makes its fur look particularly shiny. The term *points* identifies the head, ears, feet and tail. In *colourpoint* cats, such as Siamese of Colourpoint Longhairs, a second colour forms markings on the points against the background of the basic colour of the fur. *Spotted* cats have stripes broken up into separate spots. *Agouti* refers to the basic colour between the stripes of a tabby, while *ticking* describes a coat whose hairs are coloured at the tips.

Breeding a certain type of cat with the object of developing a particular fur colour or body structure sometimes results in significant health problems, the worst being serious skeletal malformations, such as the absence of a tail in a few breeds such as a the Japanese Bobtail and the Manx cat. Genetically, in certain cases this leads to infertility, as for instance with homozygous Manx cats whose young die at the embryonic stage. Only hybrids survive and are born tailless, as planned. However, they also develop a very deformed spine, so that their back looks extremely crooked and increases the jolting,

The luminous colour of the eyes of pedigree cats only develops after a few months

Right: A Chartreuse kitten whose coat and eyes have not yet developed their definite colour.

hopping walk of the Manx cat. In addition, Manx cats often suffer from polydactyly (more than the normal number of digits), a hereditary defect which also occurs in humans. Other breeds of cats suffering from polydactyly are immediately disqualified from competitions so they will never be able to win a

prize, even though this defect, caused by the same hereditary factors as determine the pigmentation of the skin, does not really affect the general health of the cat.

Many white cats with blue eyes – especially Persian cats – are deaf. When two white, blue-eyed cats are mated, the risk of producing deaf kittens is very high, but the deep blue colour of the eyes is passed to them. The risk of deafness can be reduced by mating bright white, blue-eyed Persians with Persians of another colour. The incidence of white cats with blue eyes is less frequent but they will not be deaf.

Living with deaf cats is not such a problem as it might seem because deaf cats have

learned to rely on their other senses. They often appreciate their owner's company more than other cats and find it quite easy to compensate for their lack of hearing by other means. But it is neither necessary nor desirable to produce generations of deaf cats in order to enjoy the sight of a beautiful animal. Animal protection societies welcomed the fact that since 1986, breeding animals which involves pain to the animal has been forbidden. But the deafness of white, blue-eyed cats is still a contentious issue. The debate centres around whether their deafness is a physical damage which prevents them from leading a normal life.

Longhaired cats

Persian cats

Persian cats have been popular for hundreds of years: similar longhaired cats were illustrated in China in the 12th century. In the following centuries they spread throughout Europe and the USA. Developed from the Turkish Angora cat, Persian cats have the following coatcolours: black, white with blue or orange-coloured eyes, blue and red Persians, cream, tabby, tortoiseshell and bi-colour.

Persians are very quiet animals and their long hair make them very easy to tell apart from other cats. Also typical is the snub nose and distinctive ruff or mane round the neck. Persians have very bushy tails and large round paws.

The colour of the fur is so very varied that it is impossible to list them all separately. At first Persians were blue, white or black but now over 50 colours and colour combinations have been bred. In addition, the family of Persians also includes *colour-points*, such as the Persian illustrated here.

Their quiet, domestic personality differs greatly from that of the ordinary house-cat. Persians prefer staying indoors to wandering about and hunting small prey. They love being groomed and brushed which is very necessary because of their long fur.

Persians are very friendly and sociable. They enjoy a leisurely pace of life and play less excitedly than ordinary house cats. Because of their quiet, easy-going personality, they are among the most popular pedigree cats, in spite of the fact they need to be brushed several times a day. This is very important in order to prevent their beautiful, thick, soft fur becoming matted.

Originally Persians were mainly bred in white but today they also exist in tabby and other colours

These elegant, majestic creatures must be brushed both in the direction of the growth of the hair and also at right angles to the body – the long hair make this possible and it will facilitate the removal of loose hair. It may also be necessary to use scissors to cut off any knots or matted hair which cannot be disentangles.

One of the pleasantest characteristics of the Persian is its soft, quiet voice – even cat who have not been neutered have a low voice.

These beautiful Persians are now bred in over 50 colour variations

*Colourpoint
Longhairs
are similar
to Persians
while the
mask is
inherited
from the
Siamese*

Turkish Van

The first Van-cats arrived in Britain from Turkey in 1955 and have been recognized as a breed since 1969. They originate from the region near Lake Van in eastern Turkey. They are very lively and have a distinctive quality which is very unusual in cats: they are not afraid of water. In fact they swim very well and they

The Turkish Van has beautiful markings above the eyes and a pink-tipped nose, both characteristic of the breed

love bathing in warm water, ideally with a temperature of 38° C (100° F), the same as their body temperature).

They are white with a reddish bushy tail which may have darker red rings. They have reddish chestnut markings above the eyes, separated by a strip of white fur.

Their large, upward-pointing ears are larger than those of Persian cats. Their hair is not as long but very soft and – because they have no undercoat – they need very

little care and attention. According to the standard, they should be snow-white without any yellowish markings in the fur. They have a stocky build, long body and rather delicate paws, and a discreet, beautiful ruff.

The head has a triangular shape with a rather long nose with a pretty pink tip. The pads on their paws are similarly pink.

Turkish Vans are very intelligent and have a large appetite. Because of their live-

ly personality, they should be allowed to go outdoors. As house cats, they are very robust and resistant and they enjoy going out even when the weather is very cold. They need plenty of exercise and, being very adventurous, they love exploring fields and gardens.

It is a great advantage that they like water and, being affectionate, they will allow you to wash them. However, they should be dried thoroughly afterwards. Although they are quite capable of coping with the cold as they have to in their native country, drying them not only makes them feel warmer but it also makes their fur beautifully shiny.

The chestnut-red markings above the eyes are separated by a white blaze

*Balinese cats
are similar
to Siamese
except that
their hair is
much longer*

Balinese

These longhaired cats are the result of a spontaneous mutation of Siamese cats which were born with fur that was too long. In the 1950s American breeders concentrated on this feature and began to breed 'longhaired Siamese' deliberately.

At first this mutation to longhair was considered undesirable and the breeding of Balinese cats stopped.

It was only in 1963 that these cats were recognised as a breed in the United States, while in Europe recognition was not granted until the 1980s.

Balinese cats are similar to Birmans and Colourpoint Longhairs but less stocky, medium sized and very slender, muscular yet very lithe.

This particular feature reflects their close relationship to Siamese cats. The triangular shaped head, long nose, long neck, slender long legs and coloured points – the dark markings on the head, ears, legs and tail – are clearly features they have inherited from their Siamese ancestors. So are the pointed, upright ears and the longer hind legs which make the back part of their body higher than the front and give Balinese cats their distinctive, elegant upright gait. They have very delicate paws and a long, bushy plume-like tail. Their ermine-like hair does not become matted as easily as that of Persian cats. However, it should still be brushed regularly to ensure that it remains shiny.

There are over 20 colour variations including seal point (cream to creamy-brown background with brownish markings on the face, paws and nose), blue point (bluish white fur with deep blue markings and slate-coloured nose-tip), chocolate point (ivory-coloured fur, light brown nose and chocolate brown markings), lilac point, and tabby point.

In temperament Balinese are very similar to Siamese although their voice is not quite as piercing and penetrating. Because they are gregarious, sociable and lively they love playing with people and resent being left on their own. They are striking in appearance and extremely intelligent.

In the USA,Balinese with some colourings are known as Javanese.

Turkish Angora

These beautiful cats are related to the Turkish Van and they are celebrated for their striking snow-white fur without any markings. Nowadays, they are also bred in a wide range of colours, although the pure white Turkish Angora cats are still the most popular among British and American breeders.

Angora cats have been exported to Western Europe since the 16th century, but they are now also bred in Britain, the rest of Europe and the United States. They have orange or blue eyes. Their silky hair grows without any undercoat so that it becomes less easily matted than a Persian for instance, and is therefore easier to look after. The soft ruff like a round collar, pointed ears and wavy-haired tale give it a striking appearance. They also a distinctive pale pink nose-tip and pads.

Angora cats are fine-boned with delicate paws. Other distinctive features of Angoras are its long back, sturdy legs and triangular-shaped head. It is alert, graceful and agile in its movements, and in its combination of power and grace it is similar to Turkish Van cats. In other respects it more closely resembles the Persian.

Angoras are extremely affectionate and sensitive and being very playful, making excellent pets. They love wandering around outdoors.

The pink paw pads, nose tip and ears are typical of Angora cats and they are well displayed in this magnificent specimen

A lightly ticked red (sorrel) Somali with a soft ruff

Somali

The Somali was developed as a result of a genetic mutation similar to that which led to the 'longhaired Siamese' or Balinese breeds. In this case it is longhaired mutant of the Abyssinian. Somali cats have been recognized as a breed in the Europe and USA since the 1970s, the first Somali society being founded in 1972. The

A ruddy coloured Somali, bearing a strong resemblance to a lynx

cat is bred in the usual Somali colour known as ruddy, and red, known as sorrel. Like other Abyssinians, it is now also bred in a variety of other colours such as blue and fawn, but these are not officially recognised in Britain. They are medium-sized and powerful, their long hair giving them their distinctive sleekness. A striking feature of many of these cats is their ticked hair, with contrasting markings at the end of each hair which only appears in adult cats. Somali cats with ruddy coloured hair have black ticking, while those with red fur have chocolate brown tickings. Red, brown or blue hair with darker ticking in the same colours are also found. Somali cats with a small ruff and long fur on the hind legs – known as socks – are particularly beautiful.

The large male Somali cats can look almost resemble lynxes, while their colouring and thick bushy tail gives them a fox-like appearance. With their very hairy ears and large, almond-shaped, greenish-yellow eyes, they are extraordinarily beautiful. Another striking feature of Somali cats is the very dark markings above the ears which often extend like a line towards the ears.

Somali cats are very rare and the more beautiful the animal the more expensive it is. They are very playful, affectionate and sociable and their voice can be described as very pleasant. They have an equable, affable temperament and make very agreeable companions, showing great interest in their surroundings.

A blue Somali cat surveys its surroundings

Ragdoll

Ragdoll cats are a very recent breed. The first was bred as recently as the 1960s by crossing a white longhaired female Persian cat and a male Birman. The very thick, soft, semi-long hair is slightly longer round the neck and giving the appearance of a beard. Another typical characteristic of the Ragdoll is the thick fur on the front legs, making them look sturdier and silky.

Ragdoll cats have a rounded, plush-like body, a round face with full cheeks, and their large oval eyes, usually blue, which contrast beautifully with their fawn, ivory or greyish-blue hair. Their colourpoint or bi-colour colouring with contrasting light and dark hair, a mask on their face, and dark ears and tail, give them a very attractive appearance.

The ragdoll effect is even stronger in the mitted Ragdoll, which has dark hair set off by white paws which look like little shoes, a white chest, 'bib' and chin.

As well as looking like cuddly toys, Ragdoll cats behave like them, in that they go limp when they are picked up. They love to be cuddled, hugged and squeezed because they are very affectionate. They look quite large because of their soft, thick, silky fur.

Ragdoll cats are only fully grown after three years. The same is true of the markings on their coat and in particular the dark mask which stands out against the lighter ground colour of their coat

which is very soft and silky and they love being around people. It is very important to play with these cats because they are very lively and sociable. They must be brushed and combed regularly because their fur becomes easily matted.

Ragdoll cats belong to the group of late developers and they only become fully mature at the age three years. This means that they only acquire their definitive colouring at the same age.

Norwegian Forest Cat

*The
Norwegian
Forest Cat
has a very
strong, wild,
muscular
appearance*

The wild ancestors of the Norwegian Forest Cat were originally native from the forests and fjord regions in Norway. There they were gradually domesticated by the local farmers who called them Norsk Skaukatt. The Norwegian Forest Cat has been recognized as standard in Norway and Sweden since 1972 and internationally (FIFé) since 1976.

*It has a bushy
tail, a very
thick coat with
a water-
repellent
topcoat, and
longer hair on
the hind legs*

Norwegian Forest Cats still show traces of their wild origins: they look very strong, with a magnificent ruff, impressive whiskers and beautiful socks on the hind legs. This gives them the appearance of a wild cat although of course they no longer are. Their long hair must be brushed and combed regularly because of their thick, dense undercoat which protects them against the intense cold. These cats are most beautiful in winter when their winter coat grows even longer and thicker than in summer.

They are quiet, gentle cats, friendly and sociable. They are also known for their vigilance, resistance, courage and liveliness. But above all, they are famous for their fantastic climbing and balancing skills, their affectionate nature and their gentleness. They need plenty of space to romp about and exercise, because they are not really house cats. More than any other breed, the Norwegian forest cat needs to live a 'wild' life.

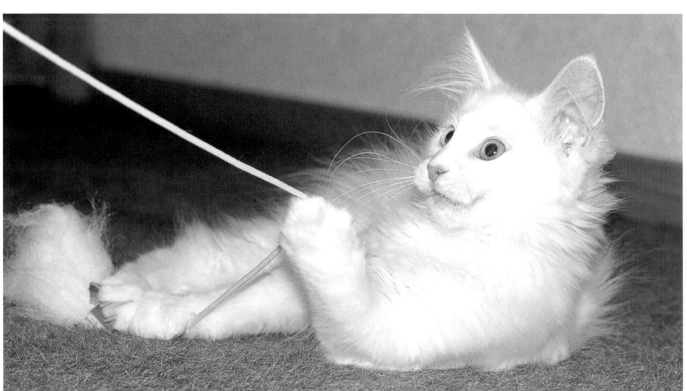

Maine Coon

The Maine Coon is a particularly large, heavy breed of cat which has been bred in the USA for over 100 years and shown since 1860. The Maine Coon owes part of its name to the State of Maine and the other part to the word 'raccoon'. Indeed, there are some similarities between the two animals: the Maine Coon is very strong and long and can weigh as mush as 15 kg (33 pounds). It has a powerful, broad chest, a smallish, angular head and pointed, bushy-haired ears. The mouth and nose are small like the head, compared to the very muscular body. The thick-set neck is adorned with a splendid ruff and the fur becomes increasingly long towards the back, looking like a shaggy coat round the tail and belly. The long hair on its hind legs look like little trousers. The tail is long and thick, becoming thinner towards the end, and covered with flowing hair. The eyes look very large in the small head and combined with its large size this gives the cat an impressive appearance. It is even more magnificent in winter when the hair becomes much thicker and the ruff even more marked.

Maine Coons come in all

The Maine Coon has a long thick coat which is seen in a variety of colours – here in brown …

… and here in cream

colours with speckles, spots and other kinds of markings. The colour of the eyes also varies enormously but the most striking aspect is their extraordinary luminosity. Particularly impressive are amber-coloured eyes with a pupil surrounded by a bright green ring.

The long fur which looks almost shaggy on the belly and back is easy to look after because there is no under-coat, so it does not become matted as easily as the fur of Persian cats.

Because of their very great size, many people believed that the Maine Coon was a cross between a raccoon and house cat. But there is no rational basis for this interpretation which belongs in the realm of fantasy and legend.

For a century the Maine Coon was an economically useful animal, much appreciated by farmers in the north-east of the United States for its great hunting skills, faced with which rats and mice were never safe. But the Maine Coon needs a lot of space and it would not be happy as a domestic cat in a

The Maine Coon is a wonderful hunter, in spite of its shaggy look

flat or town house. Nevertheless, it is a sociable creature and likes the company of human beings. It enjoys playing and being cuddled, and it gets on well with other cats in the house. Because of its gentle nature and patience, it is an ideal family cat, provided the space and conditions are satisfactory. It will often concentrate its affection on a single member of the family.

Shorthaired cats

Siamese cats

*Siamese cats
are easily
recognised
by their face
markings,
the narrow
head and
the pointed
ears*

Siamese cats are probably the best known pedigree breed apart from Persians. They are very slender with long legs and a beautiful mask on the face. They have deep-blue, almond-shaped eyes and ivory-coloured hair. One of the most distinctive features of the Siamese are its very large, long, pointed ears on a fairly small head. This head is long and wedge-shaped; in profile it looks like that of a medium-sized wild cat, for instance a lynx. Siamese cats have a face 'mask', the dark markings around the mouth, nose and ears which form the most distinctive feature of the breed.

Another typical feature of the Siamese is their short, dense, shiny fur which in

young cats is snow-white, the definitive colour only developing when they are fully mature. Obviously this short hair requires relatively little grooming on the part of its owner.

However, this does not mean that Siamese can be neglected, because they have a demanding, lively temperament. They are extremely sociable and devoted. They love romping about and playing wild games with people. They also like to be cuddled. Siamese are full of life and

energy and they enjoy tearing around the house.

In spite of their lively temperament, Siamese cats have one quality which is relatively rare among cats. They can taken out for a walk on a lead, because they become very attached to their owner. This character means that they are completely devoted to the people around them and therefore demand constant attention. When they think they are not receiving enough attention, they express their dissatisfaction by meowing loudly and piercingly, in the same way that dogs bark to attract their owner's attention. Being so strongly attached to the people around them, they are

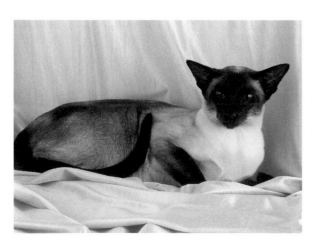

Even when posing for a photograph, the spirited personality of this Siamese still shines through

very jealous of third parties, whether cats or people.

Siamese cats are indeed native to the country from which they take their name: in Siam, the country now called Thailand, they were revered like deities before they arrived in Britain in the latter part of the 19th century.

Siamese cats are bred in a very wide range of colours: seal point, blue point, chocolate point, lilac point, tabby point, red point, cream point and tortie point. Seal points have a cream-coloured coat which turns pale brown towards the back with black-brown markings on the face, ears, legs, paws and tail. Blue-points are white and pale

blue towards the back with deep blue markings. Chocolate points have chocolate-coloured markings while lilac points, sometimes also called frost points, have bluish-lilac markings. The nose and paws are pale lilac, the markings standing out against an almost ice-blue colouring.

Tabby points have stripy markings which are particularly pronounced on the head. The ring-shaped pattern is also very visible on the legs and tail. Siamese cats are also bred with brown-black, chocolate-coloured, lilac and tortoiseshell markings as well as red markings in red points.

All Siamese cats have blue eyes which vary from a deep,

piercing blue to bright blue. In tabby points, the blue eyes are emphasised by a dark line which goes all round the eye.

Siamese cats have a long, narrow, wedge-shaped head

The blue eyes are emphasised by a black line around them

Oriental Shorthair

Oriental Shorthair is the name given to the cat breed cats whose very slender build resembles that of their nearest 'relations', the Siamese. However, they do not have the typical Siamese face mask and markings. These 'single-coloured Siamese' – a very recent standard – are bred in over 40 colours and have emerald green eyes, except for the white varieties which usually have deep blue eyes.

*Oriental Shorthairs are very
similar to Siamese cats – this
one is a chocolate spotted tabby*

In Britain the Oriental Shorthair standard includes many colour varieties, including the Oriental white (also known as the Foreign white), the Oriental blue, the Oriental red, as well as tortoiseshells and tabbies.

The Oriental white has a snow-white coat without a single coloured hair. Unlike so many white cats with blue eyes, it is not deaf . The oldest coloured Oriental Shorthair is the British Havana which has a chestnut brown coat, similar to the colour of tobacco – hence its name. Originally called Chestnut Brown Foreign Shorthair, the Havana was recognised as a standard in 1958 and re-named Havana in 1970. It has green eyes and pink pads. The rest of the body, including the tip of the nose, must be the same colour as the hair.

In 1968 breeding resulted in the development of a jet-black Oriental Shorthair, the Oriental ebony or Oriental black. The coat must be all black with no tinge of red, and the eyes are emerald green eyes. The Ebony's head is very small, even compared to that of the Siamese.

Besides these variations, the Oriental Shorthair is also bred in other colours such as blue, cinnamon, cream and caramel as well as some tabby-markings, speckled and striped. Because almost all colours are allowed, Oriental Shorthairs are judged on the uniformity and evenness of the hair colours and patterns.

In spite of being related to the Siamese, Orientals are very affectionate and quiet . They are very pleasant companions because they feel very close to the people around them and are very loyal. With their slender build and beautiful colouring, Oriental Shorhairs look extremely majestic and elegant. Their slenderness is emphasised by the evenness of their coat.

Because of their friendly nature, they are also ideal companions for other cats.

*The tobacco brown Oriental
Shorthair, developed in England,
is known as the British Havana*

Burmese

First recognized in the United States in 1936 and in England in 1952, these cats native to Burma in the far-East were established as a breed after being deliberately crossed with Siamese.

The Burmese should not be confused with the semi-long-haired 'sacred' Birman cats.

like that of the Siamese but shorter and wider. The eye colour ranges from amber to yellow and yellowish-green. Pure green eyes are considered an imperfection according to the standard. Blue Burmese have a silvery sheen on their fur and yellow eyes.

Breeders in the United States have bred a longhaired Burmese, known as Tiffany.

Burmese cats have a muscular frame and are heavier than they look

Burmese have a compact build and are very muscular. They love the company of people and are very affectionate. They enjoy climbing but they do not need a great deal of space. They love playing with people and being cuddled for hours on end.

The head of this Burmese is slightly reminiscent of a Siamese

To meet the requirements of the standard, Burmese are not permitted to display any specific Siamese features. Originally only brown, there are now also lilac, blue, red, blue-creamy-coloured and chocolate Burmese as well as torties. They are similar in build to the Siamese but they have a broader ribcage and their hind legs are a little longer than their front legs. Burmese cats have small oval paws and a long pointed tail. The head is wedge-shaped

Burmese are extremely affectionate cats and are as friendly and sociable as Siamese

Korat

The Korat is a very dainty, graceful cat with a shimmering silver-blue coat which is not too short with a slightly rounded back. They are native to the Thai province of Korat where this very beautiful cat used to be thought to bring good luck, thus becoming very popular. In ancient Thai manuscripts the Korat was described as a symbol of beauty and sparkle. In the 1950s, the Korat also became popular outside Thailand and was imported first into the United States where it was recognised as a breed in 1966 and into Europe where it was recognised in 1975.

Its graceful figure is very similar to that of the Siamese but the Korat is more powerful and muscular than its Siamese relative and is considered a medium size cat.

The head of the Korat is heart-shaped with a light nose break. The brilliant green to greeny-gold eyes stand out beautifully against the glossy hair. The large ears are strongly curved at the base and the tips are slightly rounded.

Always silver-blue, the Korat's coat is short and close to the body and its silvery sheen is due to the silver tipping of the hairs. The lips, nose pad and paw pads are dark blue and stand out a little against the colour of the fur. To win prizes, the Korat must not have any markings, speckles, shading or tabby patterns of any kind.

The large round eyes and erect ears give the Korat a very alert expression. It is very friendly, loyal and playful. But it is also jealous of other cats and demands its owner's affection completely for itself. With this reservation, it is an ideal domestic pet which loves to be cuddled and played with. Very alert and cautious, it is always busy with something.

The Korat is a beautiful cat with an elegant body, glossy coat and luminous green eyes

European Shorthair

The European Shorthair is the embodiment of the typical domestic cat. It is medium-sized, quite sturdy and relatively slenderApart from its pedigree, it does not differ in any way from hybrid domestic cats. The eyes of a European Shorthair may be blue, green , orange or yellow, and the hair is speckled with round or oblong markings which should stand out clearly against the rest of the coat. The coat is short and very thick.

Like ordinary house cats, the European Shorthair can also be bi-coloured, with white and any other colour, including black. However, there should never be more than two colours. The face

The European Shorthair is bred in countless colour combinations, such as here in cream ....

... or as here in dark brown

163

Many other colour combinations exist. The red tabby shorthair has a beautiful marbled pattern of a dark red against a red ground colour, similar to the markings of the silver tabby, with orange to hazel brown eyes. The brown tabby has eyes varying from yellow to hazel or green. Finally the striped Shorthair has well-defined stripes running from the back towards the belly, the stripes being silver, red or brown

European Shorthairs also include tortoiseshells as well as smokes. In tortoiseshells it is very important that the patches of colour should be clearly separated from each other . The red and black blotches should not merge

Bi-colour Shorthair cats with a beautiful blaze are considered particularly handsome

must also be two-toned and a white blaze is considered particularly beautiful. The eyes are usually yellow and when there are patches, the colour of the eyes should match that of the patches.

The colour combinations are very varied. They include a uniform cream – a delicate red with copper eyes – without stripes but with white patches, not forgetting the silver tabby with marbled markings: black lengthways stripes along the neck and back and black rings on the shoulders that stand out against the silver ground colour. The eyes are green or hazel.

This tabby Shorthair has a clear marble pattern on its coat

into each other but a red blaze on the face is considered very desirable. Tortoiseshells are always female (apart from a very few male cats, which are sterile). This is because the tortoiseshell gene only passes in the female line. Breeding true is therefore not easy, since female tortoiseshells are mated with black, red or cream-coloured male cats. and the litter may contain no tortoiseshells kittens at all. Ironically, when tortoiseshells spend a lot of time outside, their offspring will often be striped because, as someone remarked in the 1970s, they are not interested in the colour of the tom cat but whether they approve of it.

Even red and black Tortoiseshells are classified as three-coloured because there are two shades of red - bright red and dark red – which are taken as two different colours. The tortie-and-white has red, cream and black patches against a white ground colour. However, the white area should not cover more than half the coat.

The growth and colouring of the coat is very interesting in smoke varieties. Only the outer three-quarters of the hairs are pigmented (smoke-coloured), the rest of the hair being white or silvery. The face is covered with white sil-

very hair but so short that it does not show under the black guard hair, so that the face looks quite black and shiny. Their orange and copper eyes contrast beautifully against the ground colour.

In temperament, European Shorthairs are the same as ordinary house cats. They vary considerably; some are very playful and affectionate, while others may be shy and lethargic.

These two cats show the close relationship that exists between the European Shorthair and the 'ordinary' domestic cat

The Chartreuse is similar to the British Blue

This little kitten has large expressive eyes

Chartreuse

This cat is very similar to the British Blue Shorthair but the hair is softer and more plush-like than its relatives. The blue colouring and thick coat give the Chartreuse a special position among Shorthairs and it has its own standard in the USA, but not in Britain.

The Chartreuse owes its name to the French Carthusian monastery, the Grande Chartreuse, near Grenoble, where it was already much loved by the monks in the 16th century who are also said to have bred them.

Apart from the eyes, every parts of this cat is grey-blue. Shades range from light to dark, but with a very even colour in any individual cat. The nose pad and paw pads are the same colour as the fur. Chartreuse kittens are sometimes born with young hair which suggests that they were once crossed with a blue Persian. The cat's build is similar to that of the other Shorthairs but stockier. In spite of the fur being thick and soft, it must not be brushed too vigorously or it may lose its woolliness.

The Chartreuse is extremely robust and loves being outdoors, but it also enjoys the company of people and of other animals. The voice is soft and the period in which they are sexually receptive is very short so that they make ideal domestic cats. If trained to do so, they happily go out for a walk on a lead – whatever the weather – because they have no tendency to wander off. They are very affectionate, calm and gentle but they are also happy on their own.

The Chartreuse is very popular for its character and for its beautiful fur which contrasts beautifully with their luminous orange, copper or yellow eyes.

Russian Blue

*Even though the Russian Blue
has a short, plush coat it
should be groomed regularly
to maintain its velvety sheen*

At first sight the Russian Blue could easily be confused with a Chartreuse or a European Shorthair. But upon closer examination, the differences are quite apparent: they are strong-boned and have a long body with long, slender legs, giving them a more elegant appearance than either of the other two. They have a rather triangular head – the forehead recedes a little – with large pointed ears. The coat is soft, fine and plush-like with a silky sheen. The silvery tips on the guard hairs which stand out from the body give the coat a particular silvery shine. The eyes are almond-shaped and luminous green.

Russian Blues are said to have originated in the vicinity of the port of Archangel in Russia; from there they were imported by sailors into western Europe where they were much admired. They were first exhibited in London in 1880.

The coat should be regularly brushed so as to preserve its shine. They are easy, quiet, affectionate cats which love the company of their owners. Very sensitive and loving in nature, they are lively and outgoing, avoiding the extremes of too much exuberance and excessive lethargy.

Abyssinian

These cats originate from the region which gave them their name (present-day Ethiopia) and they are a very old breed. Tthey were first imported into Britain in 1868 and were recognized as a breed 14 years later.

Ancient Egyptian representations of cats depict a slender type of wild cat very similar to today's Abyssinian.

In build, the Abyssinian is similar to the domestic cat: medium-sized and slender but not especially graceful. Like Somali cats, the hairs have two or three bands. They are slender like the Siamese but more powerful

Abyssinians are very similar to Somali cats but with shorter hair

looking. The so-called usual colour of Abyssinians is ruddy but without stripes. The hairs are divided into several rings. The typical ticking of the individual hairs between the bright part at the root and the black tips is a reddish-brown-grey band which produces a speckled effect. Each hair can take between two and four bands

Medium-sized and slender, they have an evenly ticked coat

which, when the animal moves or the light changes, creates a variety a shadings. These are particularly beautiful in ruddy-coloured types. The coat must be combed or brushed once or twice a week.

The Abyssinian's green, yellow or hazel eyes are surrounded by a black or brown ring. It has black paw pads, a black tip of the tail and a dark pink nose. The head is narrow and long with large, pointed ears.

Usual-coloured Abyssinian mothers sometimes produce sorrel (red) kittens as well as usual-coloured kittens. In such cases the tips of the hairs are red instead of black so that the coat is ticked with red. The tail and back of the hind legs are brown and the nose and paw pads are pink.

Abyssinians love outdoor life but they are also happy to be indoors because they enjoy the company of people and like being cuddled. Being playful, they will often urge you to play with them. But they also like to sleep and they do not like to be disturbed while having a nap.

Abyssinians have not inherited any of the characteristics of their ancestors who according to ancient Egyptian legends were very belligerent and foolhardy. Abyssinians prefer to inspect the terrain first from a distance before approaching it and then exploring it. One aspect of their behaviour is very unusual: instead of sniffing new objects from a safe distance as most cats do, they check them with their paws.

Abyssinians are extremely human-friendly, companionable creatures, although initially cautious with strangers.

The same mother can produce offspring with a different coloured coats, such as these two kittens

Manx cats

Manx cats are native to the Isle of Man where they lived for many centuries and after which they were named. Their main feature is that they have no tail or merely a stump where an imposing tail would normally be expected. The hind legs are longer than the fore legs and the back is short and rounded, giving them a somewhat rabbit-like appearance and gait.

There are two types of Manx cats. The true Manx is completely tailless and known as the 'rumpy'; it has a dimple where the tail would be. The other kind, known as the 'stumpy', has a short tail consisting of a small number of vertebrae. The absence of tail caused not by docking but by a genetic mutation resulting from in-breeding (the Isle of Man was effectively isolated from the rest of Britain for many centuries). However, not all Manx kittens are born without a tail;

some have a short or even a normal tail. This is a great problem for breeders because the standard requires the complete absence of a tail, so only rumpies can win prizes.

Manx cats are bred in many colours. The body is medium-sized and rounded,

and the head and eyes are also round. They have a double coat, a thick undercoat and a shiny topcoat, giving a well-padded effect.

In spite of their hopping gait and problems with climbing and balancing, Manx cats manage very well outdoors where they are quite capable of catching mice and rats. These affectionate, loyal, friendly animals love human company and enjoy being cuddled, making them ideal house cats which are very easy to look after. But unfortunately they can suffer from spinal problems, caused by their short, curved spine and longer hind legs.

Like house-cats Manx are bred in all sorts of colour combinations

But they have no tail and hop like rabbits

Scottish Fold

From a distance the Scottish Fold looks as if it has no ears. Upon closer examination, it becomes apparent that they do have ears but these are folded forward so that they hardly visible. They have a short, thick-set almost non-existent neck which gives them an owl-like appearance. The eyes are large and round and can be almost any colour.

But when looking closer, it is noticeable that this cat has a powerful chin, strong jaw-bones and very round cheeks. The body is medium-sized, rounded and broad. It is bred in the same variety of colours as the European Shorthairs.

Because of the Scottish Fold's unusual folded ears, their shape and position are very important in the assessment of the standard: they must be wide apart, small, round at the top and tightly folded.

A cat with folded ears was already known in China many centuries ago. The story is that it was introduced into Europe by sailor, but this is unlikely to be true. The Scottish Fold is the result of a spontaneous mutation, and it was first discovered in Scotland in 1961. At first it was only bred in white but they are now bred in all colours. According to the standard, the Scottish Fold must be medium-sized with a round-ed body, a thick coat, and large round eyes set wide apart.

People who are comfort-able with the folded ears will find the Scottish Fold a very friendly cat of enormous charm which gets on well with people and animals. It loves playing with children will become very much part of the family.

*The Scottish Fold was
first discovered in 1961*

Rex Breeds

The Rex Breeds include the Cornish (or German) Rex, Devon Rex, German Rex and Oregon Rex. The most striking feature of these cats is their curly, plush-like coat which occurs in a wide range of colours. The very slender body is medium-sized, the head wedge-shaped and the

A black Rex with a curly coat

ears disproportionately large.

The breeds are the result of mutations. The Cornish Rex was discovered in Cornwall in 1950, while the Devon Rex was found in 1950. In America, the Oregon Rex was found in Oregon. Rexes with Siamese points are unofficially known as Si-Rexes.

The coat of pedigree Rex cats is very short, fine and soft without bare patches and not shaggy. The Cornish

Rexes have short, dense curly hair while the Devon has longer, waved or curly hair. The coat of Rex cats requires very little care, not needing to be brushed or combed.

But because of the coat's relative thinness, Rex cats need to be protected against extreme heat and cold. It also means that they use up more energy than other breeds to maintain their body temperature up. This increases their metabolic rate and, as a result, gives them a very large appetite. It is therefore very important for owners to take this into account when feeding their cats.

The Oregon Rex is even more slender than the other Rex breeds with a narrower head. Because of their enormous ears, they are also known as Butterfly and also because of the butterfly-shaped markings on the face.

These sometimes almost poodle-like cats are extremely friendly and affectionate with a very loud purr. They are very lively when playing and, in spite of their dainty build, are very powerful and muscular. American breeders also report that they are happy to be taken out on a leash and walk behind their owner like a little dog. However, their large appetite is often their undoing, so they need to be watched in case they become overweight.

The coat of this Rex is unusually short and it is very evident that it needs to be protected from heat and cold.
Below: A short-haired silver tabby

Japanese Bobtail

This breed is famous for its unusual, stumpy tail which has inspired its name. But unlike the Manx cat, the Japanese Bobtail has a 'normally-formed' spine and the hind legs are not longer than the front legs. This is why it walks like a cat and not like a rabbit as the Manx cat does. In Japan they are called 'Mi-Ke' and bred with three colours of fur: black, red and white. The Bobtail is also bred in bi-colours such as black and white and red and white. There are also tortoise-shell Bobtails and some with striped markings.

These cats were popular in Japan because the Japanese believed that a cat's tail was inhabited by the devil. For over 500 years this superstitious belief saved the Bobtail from the dreadful fate encountered by other cats. Being without tails they were considered harmless animals which, unlike other cats could not turn into women or raise the dead.

The stumpy tail looks more like a little ball because of the thickness of the hair which grows on it. If the tail is more than 14 cm (5½ in), the cat is no longer recognised as a Bobtail and it cannot take part in competitions. The coat is soft and silky and the head is triangular. They are very friendly and require very little care, making them excellent pets. They need to be free to go outdoors.

The Japanese Bobtail has a short tail looking like a pom-pom, which is carried upright

Exotic Shorthair

The Exotic Shorthair breed was recognised in 1966. It belongs to the group of Shorthairs and has a powerful build similar to that of house cats. Like them, it has a thick coat, a broad, muscular chest, legs of average length and a straight, horizontal back. But the snub nose, small ears, round eyes and plush, soft hair are more reminiscent of Persians. So one could almost describe these Exotic Shorthairs as short-haired Persian cats, and they were indeed developed by crossing Persians with other American Shorthair types. From its appearance, it has been nicknamed 'the teddy bear cat'.

The Exotic Shorthair makes an ideal house cat, playful but not too lively and very robust. It is happy to live indoors. Like the Persians, the Exotic Shorthair has a soft voice. Although slightly longer than that of other Shorthairs, its coat requires relatively little grooming.

Exotic Shorthairs are bred in the same variety of colours and patterns as Persian cats.

This cat has inherited its little snub nose from its Persian ancestors. The fur is very similar to that of the European Shorthair. The Exotic Shorthair makes an ideal pet because it needs very little care and is very affectionate.

Sphynx

The most striking feature of
the Sphynx is its complete
absence of hair, resulting
from a spontaneous mutation
which occurred in Canada. It
is consequently known as the
Hairless Sphynx or as the
Canadian Hairless Cat. Apart
from its absence of hair, it is
very similar to the Rex
Breeds, particularly in its
build and its disproportionately large ears. In reality the
face and body are covered
with light fuzzy hairs, very
soft with a silky sheen. While
the body temperature of
other cats is regulated by
their hair, Sphynxes compensate by developing a thicker

*Sphinxes are
a special
breed of
hairless cats
whose body
is actually
covered with
a very short
downy coat*

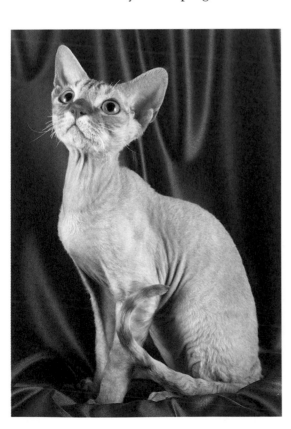

subcutaneous layer of fat
which prevents the loss of
body heat. Nevertheless, it is
better not to let Sphynxes go
out of doors.

The breed is recognised in
the USA and some European
countries but not in Britain.
The result of a breeding exercise taking advantage of an
accidental mutation, it lacks
those attractive features of
other cats which lie in the
feel and appearance of their
coats. But it is quite popular,
for instance among people

who want a cat but are allergic to cat hair. The first
Canadian Hairless Cat was
born in Ontario, Canada, in
1966, one of a black and
white cat's litter.

In spite of its apparent
fragility, the Sphynx is very
powerful and resistant. It is
not very affectionate and
does not like to be cuddled.
Its large, golden eyes, set
wide apart, are very beautiful
and will appeal to some cat
lovers. Their breeding is still
very controversial.

Whether pedigree or ordinary domestic moggies, all cats love to play

Glossary:

All about cats from A to Z

Allergy

Like humans, cats too suffer from allergies. Even certain kinds of grass can cause them to sneeze and cough while the presence of parasites on the skin can lead to strong itching and scratching.

But a much more common allergy is that of humans to to cat's hair. The fine hairs seem to get through the narrowest gaps and people allergic to cats often feel that cat hairs have got into their nose and eyes because of the strong itching. It is very hard to prevent cat hairs getting everywhere in the home and even in the beds. Those who are sensitive or allergic to dust and fluff are more likely to be allergic to cat hair than those have no other allergies. It is therefore advisable to have an allergy test before acquiring a cat.

Anaesthesia

In the case of animals, a general anaesthetic is always given even for a small operation when in the case of humans, a local anaesthetic would be given – such as for dental treatment. The reason is that animals would not remain still during the treatment and might even scratch or bite the vet.

Body temperature

A cat's normal body temperature ranges between 38.5 and 39.3° C (101.3 to 102.7° F). This is higher than humans.

Bone fractures

According to the saying, a cat has nine lives, and it is widely believed that they will always land on their feet even when they fall from a great height. Unfortunately, this is

not always true because cats do get injured and they can break bones, for instance if they fall out of the window. Minor fractures often heal on their own – after hobbling for a few days the cat's toe seems to be all right again. But more serious fractures, such as a broken thigh, should be treated surgically if necessary and fitted with a cast by the vet. This should be followed by a several weeks of rest.

Carpal pad and metocarpal pad

On a cat's front paw, the metocarpal pad is behind the toe pads and corresponds to the palm of the hand. The carpal pad is situated 2–3 cm (about an inch) further up the paw and almost looks like atrophied thumbs. Like the toe pads, these are sensitive to temperature and pressure and can secrete scent marks.

Cat flu

A feverish, highly infectious disease against which all cats must be vaccinated, even those which never go out. It is the common term for feline upper respiratory virus infection.

Cat language

The feline vocabulary consists partly of body language and also of a range of sounds to attract attention. Some examples follow. A bushy tail and enlarged pupils indicates fear. A light wagging of the tail expresses joy. When a cat's ears are erect and leaning slightly forward, they express alertness and curiosity; if the ears are laid slightly back, it is a warning; but if the ears are really laid back so they are almost flat on their head, watch out – it's about to attack! Purring can soon turn into a grumble and a growl if the cat is displeased by some-thing, while an arched back clearly shows other cats and animals that they should keep out of the way.

Cats and dogs

These two so-called arch-enemies usually get on very well after an initial period of getting used to each other. However, the first encounter between a cat and a dog is often quite stressful at first and should not last too long. People who already have a dog and are now getting a cat (or vice-versa) need not worry because with a little patience, the two animals will soon become firm friends.

Claws

The cat's sharp claws are its most important tool for grasping, holding and hunt-ing. A cat whets its claws reg-ularly on trees or a scratching pole. During this process they also remove the old, horn-like sheaths. Unless you are experienced, you should not try to trim the cat's claws because the tips contain blood vessels and nerves. It is a job best left to the vet.

The removal of claws – sometimes carried out in America on cats which live exclusively indoors – is com-pletely unnecessary and unnatural. It also makes the cat defenceless if it should go out. It is done to prevent the furniture being damaged by scratching. Instead, people should give their cat a scratching pole – and not remove an important of their anatomy.

Collar

Cat collars are used mainly to identify the cat – only a few people use a collar and lead to take their cat for a walk. (A led is however compulsory in some parts of the USA.) If the cat goes out, it is very important to that it should wear a collar with your address or telephone number. This means that, if the cat gets lost, anyone finding it will realise that it is not a stray; they may even bring it back to you or let you know what has happened to it.

Collar and lead

Not many cats are put on a lead but some breeds can be trained to it, and it can be useful in some situations. A plain collar and lead such as are used for a dog should not be used. It is much safer to use and collar and harness which goes round the neck of the cat and also round the

chest. This greatly reduces the risk of injury if the cat gets stuck in a bush or fence. A retractable lead is the best kind to use.

Constipation

Constipation may be the result of hairballs in the stomach, poor digestion, or possibly of a serious infectious disease. Try purgatives such as grass and malt paste to alleviate the condition. If the constipation persists it is advisable to take the cat to the vet.

Death of a Cat

Many cat owners do not know what to do when their cat dies. Besides the loss, pain and grief caused the cat's death, there is the added problem of what to with the corpse and where to bury it. Owners often like to bury their pet nearby but this is often forbidden for health

reasons. It is therefore best to contact the vet to arrange for its disposal.

Diarrhoea

A light diarrhoea which only lasts a couple of days is not dangerous for the cat. The best way of dealing with diarrhoea is to cleanse the digestive system by not giving it anything to eat or drink, except water. If the diarrhoea continues and is associated with vomiting, you must take the cat to the vet because it could be caused by a viral infection.

Diet

Many older and often overweight cats suffer from diabetes. If this is the case, the vet will prescribe a special diet which must be followed very carefully. But this is not as easy as it might appear and it is quite difficult to enforce when the cat only wants its usual favourite foods. Fortunately there are now ready-made, balanced diet foods which will meet your cat's dietary requirements and which are very similar to ordinary tinned cat food.

If your cat is overweight, you can try and put it on a slimming diet. All you need do is to reduce the size of the portions until you give only half the usual amount. By reducing the portions very slowly and gradually – over a period of about two months – you will be successful and the cat will lose weight.

Elizabethan Collar

This is rigid, plastic collar which are put round the cat's neck if it is injured around their eyes or ears so that it cannot scratch or lick the wounds.

Feline leukaemia virus

This is an infectious, incurable disease which is often fatal. It is vitally important that cats are vaccinated against this disease – even those which never go out.

Fever

Cats have a constant body temperature of about 38–39° C (about 100–102° F) and their body reacts to infections with fever in the same way as humans do. Weakness and heavy sweating are often

symptoms of fever. If the cat's temperature goes up by more than about 1° C (2°F), it is a sign that the cat has an internal or external infection. If the fever does not quickly come down, you should consult a vet immediately.

Taking a cat's temperature is not very easy. You will need a second person to hold the cat because it will struggle furiously when you introduce the thermometer into its anus.

Fish

Fish is a pleasant and healthy alternative to meat. This should preferably be white fish, not too oily, cooked and boned. (The common belief that cats are able to avoid swallowing the bones when eating fish is erroneous.)

Fleas

Skin rashes and severe itching are usually caused by fleas. Cat fleas cannot be passed on to humans. The fleas may fall or jump out of the fur and bite, but they do not live on humans. A flea is a dark brown, wingless insect, 2 mm (³⁄₃₂ in) long which can be seen in the cat's fur.

Flea powders are quite an effective treatment for ridding your cat of fleas. Put the cat on a newspaper and spray it with flea powder, being careful to avoid the eyes and ears. Finally brush the powder out of the cat's hair, together with the fleas. It is also advisable to spray the places where the cat sleeps and plays. Flea collars which are available from pet shops and supermarkets are also

helpful, although some cats are allergic to the flea repellent which has a fairly unpleasant smell. When dealing with a flea infestation, it is important to sweep up the fleas which have fallen out of the cat's fur and kill them. This is because the flea powder and flea collar do not kill the fleas but merely make them fall out of the cat's fur; after which they continue to live on the floorboards, carpets and furnishings so that they will re-infest your cat as soon as it gets near a nest.

Food bowl

Each cat needs its own food bowl. It should be placed on a mat or a newspaper in a quiet corner of the kitchen because cats love playing with their food and usually drag it out of the bowl before eating it.

Hair loss

The new growth of hair in spring also means that a larger number of old hairs die and are discarded. This process of moulting is perfectly normal for a cat. But serious hair loss can be caused by stress and illness. Scabies, fungal skin infections and vitamin deficiencies may also lead to partial or complete loss of hair. In this case, the cat should immediately be taken to the vet and examined to establish the cause of the condition.

Hairballs

Hairballs are the result of hairs ingested while grooming themselves. They are compressed balls of hairs which cannot be digested by the cat and therefore remain in the stomach. These hairballs may become so hard that, in serious cases, they can paralyse the entire digestive system, causing constipating and frequent vomiting. The best way to prevent this happening is frequent brushing and combing, especially in the case of long-haired cats. Making fresh grass available to the cat will helps bring up the ingested hairs. Malt paste, available from the vet, is also helpful.

Haw

The haw is a third eyelid which moves diagonally across the cornea or surface of the eyeball. If the haw covers the eye partly or completely, it means that the cat is not healthy and it should be examined by the vet.

Heart

In a healthy cat the heart beats 110 to 130 times per minute, while it takes 20 to 25 breaths per minuteBoth figures are more rapid than in humans.

Jacobson's organ

This is a small organ in the nasal cavity which stores up scents and which is used by the cats to create a scent map of their surroundings. This organ also contains all the scent memories which cats need to survive. It is this organ which helps them to smell the food they eat and to identify the scent produced by other animals.

Jaundice

Jaundice is a unpleasant illness and a serious indication of liver disorder whose symptoms include listlessness and loss of appetite, dirty smelly faeces, lacklustre eyes, a shaggy coat and a yellow to orange mucous membrane.

Laxative

If your cat is constipated, never give it laxatives intended for humans, such as castor oil. These could seriously injure your cat. Instead, you can give it a small amount of olive oil by adding it to the cat's food, which will normally alleviate the condition. As soon as the cat's motions become more liquid and a slight diarrhoea develops, you must discontinue the addition of oil or butter to its food. If the cat continues to be constipated in spite of

daily administrations of oil, it should be taken to the vet.

Life expectancy

The life expectancy of cats is between 14 and 20 years. Although these elegant creatures seem to be remarkably robust, as they grow older they suffer from the usual complaints, aches and pains associated with old age. They become more sensitive to infectious diseases and seem to enjoy rest more than when they were young. In fact, old cats suffer from the same problems as humans: digestive problems, kidney problems and skin disorders.

Litter tray

This is a plastic tray, available in pet shops and many supermarkets, which is filled with cat litter, a special material which clumps when in contact with urine or faeces. It also has deodorising properties. It is very important that the tray is kept scrupulously clean so that the cat does not look elsewhere to relieve itself. All clumped litter and solid matter should be removed twice a day, using a small shovel. The tray should be emptied, washed and disinfected at least once a week and filled with new litter.

Lymphosarcoma

This is a malignant growth of the lymphoid elements

183

which affects the lymphatic glands, spleen, kidneys and intestines. Cats suffering from this type of cancer are usually between four and eight years old. The symptoms are vomiting, diarrhoea or constipation. Vets can

remove the cancer surgically but in spite of this many cats die after a few weeks.

Marking
In order to mark its territory, a cat will spray urine round the area they claim as their territory. This indicates to other cats that it is a no-go area.

Matted fur
Longhaired cats such as Persians often suffer from a matted coat if they are not brushed and combed regularly by their owner. If the fur is

so badly matted that the hair is completely tangled and full of knots and clumps, the only solution is to cut it with scissors. In the case of short-haired cats, matted hair and knots are often the result of a lack of grooming by the cat itself. This may be caused by a variety of reasons such as neglect or loneliness. Try and gently disentangle the knots and clumps using a comb, and scissors where necessary.

Medication
Medications which help humans get better are often poisonous for cats. A cat should only have medicines prescribed to it by the vet.

Milk
Milk causes diarrhoea in adult cats and should only be

given as a rare treat – even though all cats love it. Small kittens should not be given cow's milk because it is not particularly good for them. It is best to give cats milk preparations designed for them.

Neutering and Spaying
Neutering and spaying is the removal of the cat's reproductive organs. This is absolutely necessary because there are already too many unwanted cats in existence, and animal shelters find it hard to cope with the number of homeless cats. When the cat reaches sexual maturity, the operation is performed under general anaesthetic. It makes cats more home-loving and affectionate, and much quieter, as well as less likely to wander. Moreover, a neutered male will no longer spray its surroundings so that it is no longer necessary to put up with the unpleasant smell and irritation of that distressing habit. Female cats no longer run the risk of pregnancy and cancer of the womb.

Oestrus
This is the word for being on heat, meaning the period during which the female cat is sexually receptive and therefore ready to mate. Unlike bitches, female cats can be on heat several times a year and during this period

All cats love a good stretch

they will rub against chair legs and roll on the floor, crying noisily and incessantly for a mate. It is very difficult for people to live with a cat on heat if the cat cannot go out. But it is equally distressing for the cat if it cannot find a mate.

Parasites in the ear
These parasites are small arachnids which invade the auditory canal and cause a lot of itching. A cat suffering from this type of parasite is always scratching its ear and shaking its head. If the infestation is serious, it will suffer from cramp-like attacks or behave as if it was drunk. It is important to go the vet who will be able to advise on what to do.

Purring and whiskers
Cats purr when they feel happy. In order to do so, they use their whiskers which are also an organ of balance.

Pedigree cats
This term describes registered cats of all the recognised breeds. Each pedigree has its own name, a standard with a particular classification number. For instance '20' refers to the brown-striped European Shorthair and its external features such as the colour of the eyes, markings on the fur, size and shape of the body.

When a cat is registered,
the registration document records its date of birth, its ancestry for at least four generations, the breeder's name, the owner's name and the kitten's official name (which often includes the name of the cattery where it was bred). An unregistered cat is not a pedigree cat, even if it is of a recognised breed.

Picking up a cat
A cat mother may pick up its kittens by the scruff of the neck, but a human should never do so because it could cause serious damage to the animal's muscles. A cat or kitten should always be picked up by placing one hand under its stomach and the other under its behind.

Rabies
Rabies occurs everywhere in the world except in Britain and Australia. It is an incurable disease and a cat which has it will die an agonising death over several days.

Therefore cats which may encounter it must be vaccinated against it. A rabid cat poses a serious threat to humans as well as to other animals.

Raising their head
Cats greet each other – and humans too – by slightly raising their head. If they nudge you with their forehead, it is their way of asking you to stroke and tickle them.

Scratching pole
It is recommended to get cats used to a scratching pole from a very early age. This scratching pole should be as tall as possible so that the cat can also climb up it. There are many designs at various prices, or you could also make your own for your cat.

Sneezing
Two or three sneezes in a row is quite normal in a cat. If it sneezes continuously and also refuses to eat, it should be taken immediately to the vet.

Teeth and gums
Rare is the cat owner who has ever succeeded in cleaning his cat's teeth, even with the special toothbrush developed for the purpose. Unless your cat is one of the rare ones which allows you to clean its teeth, you will need a helper to hold the cat down while

you clean its teeth. But do be careful, cats bite and it hurts! If there is plaque or tartar, scratch it off to remove it. It usually comes off quite easily. If the tartar is too thick to remove it or the cat will not let look at its mouth, it is best to go to the vet.

Ticks

Cats sometimes pick up ticks when they go outside. If you notice any, brush your cat immediately; whilethey are still loose on the fur, they fall off quite easily when brushed. But if the ticks have had time to burrow their way under the skin, you will have to pull them out very carefully, or the head will remain under the skin and continue to live there. If you put a little oil on the tick, it stops them from breathing and it will be easier to remove them. However, do not underestimate the danger of ticks because they can also transmit dangerous bacterial and viral infections such as meningitis to humans.

Vaccinations

Between the ages of 8 and 12 weeks, cats must be vaccinated against feline infectious enteritis, respiratory viral infection (cat flu) and feline leukaemia virus (FeLV). Four weeks later, they are given a second injection of these vaccines. Cats which go out a lot should also be vaccinated against rabies in countries other than Britain or Australia, Feline Immuno-deficiency Virus (FIV) and Feline Infectious Peritonitis (FIP).

Vitamins

Pregnant cats, cats which are being wormed and cats which have been put on a diet should be given additional vitamins, because vitamin deficiency inevitably leads to general weakness and a lacklustre coat. Only give your cat special vitamins prescribed by the vet. Also give it liver once or twice a week.

Vomiting

All cats are sick now and again, even when healthy. Do not worry if the cat vomits to bring up swallowed hairballs or if vomiting is the result of eating too quickly. But consult vet if the condition persists. The vomiting could be caused by a kidney disorder, a serious stomach upset or aninfectious disease. But cats most commonly vomit after eating grass, which they do to bring up the indigestible hairballs from the stomach.

Weight-watching

It is very hard to keep a cat long enough on the scales to read its weight. Instead, weigh it inside the cat carrier, then subtract the weight of the carrier. Alternatively, hold the cat and stand on the scales yourself, then deduct your own weight. Normal, adult cats weigh between 3 and 6 kg (6½ to 13 lbs), but it is quite normal for smaller breeds not to exceed 2–3 kg (4½–6½ lbs).

Cats are happy animals which love to play

Like all cats, this one is clearly very curious and looks at everything that moves

Cats adore soft, fluffy blankets and cushions

Always make sure that your cat has enough opportunities to play

A very cuddly cat